MINERALS AND MEN

MINERALS AND MEN

an exploration of the world of minerals and metals, including some of the major problems that are posed

revised and enlarged edition

JAMES F. McDIVITT

GERALD MANNERS

Published for RESOURCES FOR THE FUTURE, INC. by The Johns Hopkins University Press, Baltimore and London

This book is one of RFF's studies in energy and nonfuel
minerals, which are directed by Hans H. Landsberg. It has been
written and designed especially for students and general readers
who are interested in the world of minerals. While drawing
heavily on an earlier edition published in 1965, the current
book has been expanded and revised to reflect the many
changes that have occurred since that time. The figures were
drawn by Frank and Clare Ford. The book was edited by Vera
W. Dodds and Charlene Semer.

RFF editors: Mark Reinsberg, Joan R. Tron, Ruth B. Haas,
Margaret Ingram

Cover courtesy British Steel Corporation

Preface

THIS is a book for interested, but not expert, readers who want to know more about the nonfuel minerals that are so important in our modern economy. In their final forms most of the metals and other mineral materials are familiar enough in hundreds of everyday uses, but many of the factors that underlie their availability and determine their cost are not nearly so familiar.

It is with these less known factors that this book deals. It is not a geological treatise nor yet a wholly economic one, but blends some geological information with monetary requirements, some technological concepts with environmental problems and foreign trade implications. It looks broadly at minerals as they affect peoples' lives wherever they may live. Thus the book provides background against which readers can weigh the facts and issues that bear upon policy decisions that must be made now and in the future by government and industry.

One of the most useful features of this study, I believe, is the way in which it gives economic perspective to physical facts. Geologically, the minerals used by man are abundant beyond measure. They are the stuff the earth is made of. But most of this material is in such low concentration or lies so deep that it cannot be looked upon as an economic source of minerals today, even though in recent years large-scale mining techniques have enabled the industry to produce marketable metals from progressively lower grade minerals.

But the fact that the minerals are there reminds us that we do live in a finite world and that in resource matters there are few absolutes: wise decisions characteristically are compromises. Seldom can we afford full utilization of a river, a mine, a fishery, or a forest. As demand for minerals grows and with it an accompanying demand for energy, and as environmental concerns continue to affect decision making, costs become higher and quality can be impaired. Yet, faced with shortage or increasing cost, enterprising people with a diversified technology and a gift for adaptation often can find substitutes. And sometimes hitherto unknown areas of mineral supply can be found. Whenever the pressures of economic advances and population growth grind hard on the global resource base, individual and social adjustments may be expected to intervene. All these observations characterize the minerals sector of the economy, where new discoveries, new technology, substitutions, shifting relative costs,, and changes in demand and supply are in continuous play on the changing scene.

This revised edition of a book first published in 1965 has been thoroughly updated to bring into focus a decade of changing technological, environmental, and political considerations as they affect the role of minerals in the world of today and tomorrow. While retaining its original theme and structure, the authors have drawn on more recent RFF and other research in specialized areas. At the same time, reflecting the shrinking world we live in, they have brought to the present book a far more global view of mineral problems than was attempted in the earlier edition, which was restricted largely to the United States scene.

James F. McDivitt, author of the 1965 edition of *Minerals and Men,* was at that time associate professor of mineral economics at the Pennsylvania State University; he is now director of UNESCO's Field Science Office for Southeast Asia, in Indonesia. In this new edition he has collaborated with Gerald Manners, who revised and updated the original book. Both authors have contributed fresh insights to the revision, drawing upon their individual knowledge of the minerals field. Professor Manners, author of the recent book *The Changing World Market for Iron Ore, 1950–1980,* is reader in Geography at University College London, University of London, and was a visiting scholar at Resources for the Future during 1964–1965.

Joseph L. Fisher, President
February 1974   Resources for the Future

Acknowledgments

THE AUTHORS wish to acknowledge the help they have had from a number of people who assisted them in resolving the problems that arise in revising, enlarging, and updating a book first published nearly a decade ago. At that time the world's mineral resources were less burdened by the increasing demands of an industrial society than they are today. But the basic elements—of exploration, production, technology, and the play of supply and demand—remain much the same. Two additional elements have come to the forefront in recent years. They are the growing awareness of citizen responsibility to preserve environmental quality, and the recognition that actions of less industrially developed countries can be as vital to the working of a reasonably balanced world economy as can the actions of fully industrialized nations. Both of these concepts have wrought many changes in men's attitudes toward the current and prospective position of minerals in our society.

With regard to all of these areas, we are grateful for the perceptive and careful review of David B. Brooks and Peter Andrews, of Canada's Department of Energy, Mines and Resources, in which the former is director of research in the office of the economic adviser, and the latter is acting head of the Futures Research Section, Mineral Development Sector. Similarly, we thank Jared E. Hazleton, associate professor of economics at the Lyndon B. Johnson School of Public Affairs, The University of Texas at Austin, for his review of an early draft of the manuscript. The overall support of Resources for the Future—in particular, of Joseph L. Fisher, Hans H. Landsberg, Sam H. Schurr, and Mark Reinsberg, who were responsible for bringing this book into being —has been of inestimable value. Two of RFF's energy and minerals staff, Frederick J. Wells and Leonard L. Fischman, contributed greatly to the final checking of current data. Lastly, we owe much to the skillful editing of Vera Dodds and Charlene Semer, whose efforts, we think, have helped to produce a text that combines the views of both authors.

James F. McDivitt
Gerald Manners

February 1974

Contents

List of tables

List of figures

List of plates

ONE · THE PLACE OF MINERALS IN MODERN SOCIETY:

in which the general organization of the book is discussed and some of the unique characteristics of minerals are examined

I AN INTRODUCTION TO THE MINERAL WORLD

SINCE before the dawn of recorded history man has looked to the earth for materials from which to build his shelters and to make his tools and utensils. Over the centuries this gouging and scratching at the surface to find clay, flint, bright stones, or occasional pieces of native copper evolved into a burrowing beneath the surface in the broadening search for mineral materials. As history has progressed, the need for minerals has increased, and the search has gone on. Indeed, the passage of time has seen the use of an ever-increasing array of mineral raw materials, in ever-expanding quantities, for a multitude of purposes—materials which man recovers from the ends and depths of the earth.

Today the mineral products of the earth are so commonly used that they affect every aspect of our lives, and today the average American is the largest consumer of minerals the world has ever known. Each year he uses, or has used on his behalf, a remarkable variety of minerals in quantities that would overwhelm him if his quota for the year were to be dumped on his doorstep on New Year's morning! In 1970, per capita consumption of minerals in the United States (the average amount of material devoted directly or indirectly to each person) included nearly 1,400 pounds (620 kilograms) of steel—a man's car perhaps; 44 pounds (20 kilograms) of aluminum—for containers, kitchenware, house siding, etc.; 20 pounds (9 kilograms) of copper—much of this used in the electrical industry; less than a pound (0.4 kilogram) of tin—one-third of which went into tin cans; and a host of other less easily identifiable metals.[1]

[1] Throughout this book, the U.S./Imperial measures are usually followed in parentheses by their equivalent measures in the International System of Units. *Tons* are *metric tons* (2,204 pounds) except where they apply to *deadweight tons,* when they are long tons (2,240 pounds).

This is by no means the end. Few of us have any idea of the amount of fuel we consume in a year. The 3.4 tons of crude oil allocated to every American on a per capita basis and used for transport, industrial, and heating purposes, may not come as a surprise. But less directly that same person consumes (in oil equivalent tons) a further 2.5 tons of natural gas and 1.6 tons of solid fuels. This latter figure is equivalent to nearly 2.3 tons per person of actual coal and lignite, over 60 percent of which is converted into electricity, and much of the rest is used to produce each person's 1,400 pounds of steel. In addition to these minerals, each American uses some 440 pounds (200 kilograms) of salt, only a very small part of which takes the form of food seasoning; nearly 70 pounds (over 30 kilograms) of sulfur, the bulk of which is used to produce sulfuric acid, which in turn goes into fertilizer production; and over 4 tons of sand and gravel, most of which is used by the construction industry for buildings and highways. The list goes on, and the quantities continue to mount.

FUNDAMENTAL CONCERNS • The world's appetite for minerals is great, and is steadily increasing. The last half-century has seen mankind consume more mineral resources than were used in the whole of previous history, and that consumption has been concentrated in a mere handful of wealthy nations, particularly the United States. This gargantuan appetite for raw materials, and the questionable ability of the earth to continue satisfying it, provide the starting point for any consideration of minerals. The possible exhaustion of useful mineral supplies has long been a matter of concern for thinking man. For these resources upon which we are drawing in increasing quantities are nonrenewable resources. The stock which is in the earth today must serve all people for all time. Each ton of iron ore, copper, or gravel taken from the earth and put into use reduces by one ton the amount of new material available for future users. This is not to say that the metals derived from minerals are irrevocably destroyed; we know from the thermodynamic principle of conservation of matter that matter is only transferred, but in man's process of conservation and consumption, minerals and metals enter into a process that to one degree or another is irreversible. As Erich Zimmerman has said of minerals:

They are wasting assets. They are completely consumed in use if they are fuels; they are at least partially dissipated if they are minerals other than fuels. Therefore the questions, "How large are the reserves? How much is left in the ground? What will happen when it is gone?" are vital questions of life and death. For ours is truly a mineral civilization, a civilization which stands and falls on its capacity to produce staggering amounts of some minerals and varying quantities of many others. (48, p. 439)

In more recent years public concern about the mineral industries has broadened into two further areas. One centers on the pollution caused by mining and its associated smelting operations. The dumping of huge quantities of waste materials into the sea and lakes; the passing of noxious chemicals into rivers and streams; the emission of poisonous gases into the atmosphere—these are industrial practices that have gone on for generations. But lately the increasing scale of mining and smelting operations, and with it the growing magnitude of the associated pollution, have alarmed a world growing more and more conscious of its environmental heritage and responsibilities. As part of this concern, particularly in highly urbanized countries, conflicts have arisen between those who would use certain lands for mining and those who would deny their use for this purpose. Minerals are not selective in their location; sometimes they may lie close to a rapidly growing urban area. It is in cases like these that disagreements arise. When is it appropriate to reserve the land for mineral extraction, and when is it appropriate to give preference to alternative land uses? Wherever such conflicts have arisen, they have generated a new and vigorous attitude questioning the grounds on which land use decisions are made.

Each of these concerns—one relating to resource adequacy, the other to environmental quality—is given attention and perspective in the course of the following chapters.

THE CHANGING IMAGE OF MINING • Nature has dictated that many minable mineral deposits occur far from man's normal habitat, in mountainous areas where the rocks are highly contorted and shot through with faults and veins. The geological environment which particularly favors mineral concentration is seldom well-suited to other types of economic activity. The land may be able to support grazing but very often little in the way of crops can be grown; transport is restricted to the major valleys; and any economic activity that does develop tends to be based almost entirely on local natural resources. In some such areas one can see the equivalent of a "one crop" economy, in which minerals are the crop and the sole reason for man's permanent presence there. Such mining communities tend to be somewhat isolated and consequently the average person knows relatively little about mining as an activity. He may, in fact, instinctively shun close acquaintance with an occupation which traditionally has been carried out beneath the surface of the earth. Mining in former times involved hard hand labor in a dangerous and unhealthy environment. The Greeks and Romans operated many of their mines with slaves and prisoners. Lewis Mumford notes: "Apart from the lure of prospecting, no one entered the mine in civilized states until relatively modern times except as a prisoner of war, a criminal, or a slave. Mining was not regarded as a humane art; it was a form of punishment; it combined the terrors of the dungeon with the physical exacerbation of the galley." (36, p. 67)

Even during the Middle Ages, however, the mineral industry began to change, and in many respects anticipated important developments that would be adopted later by other industries. Agricola, writing over 400 years ago, noted that " . . . many people hold the opinion that the metal industries are fortuitous and that the occupation is one of sordid toil, and altogether a kind of business requiring not so much skill as labour." (1, p. 2) But Agricola could not agree with the "many people" to whom he referred, for during his time mining was a progressive industry which was held in considerable respect. There still remain strong traces of the guilds and societies set up by the miners in the metal belts of Europe at that time, when the practice of mining was a more scientific operation than most other industrial activities. Indeed, many of the important industrial advances in the past were orginally developed for use in the mines. Steam engines were first used for ventilation and for pumping water from mines; railroads were first developed for the transportation of heavy loads of ore.

New and important advances are still being made in the mineral industries, but it is only rarely that they come to public attention. The development of the Geiger counter, which permitted the uranium rush of the 1950s, changed the prevailing image of the prospector from bearded adventurer with pick and burro to a smooth-faced technician with counter and jeep; and at the same time it breathed new life into the old, romantic notion that mining is an activity in which some can "get rich quick."

Even as the gold prospector has given way to the man with the Geiger counter, the whole mining industry has undergone enormous changes over the past decades. In the new picture we see a series of industries recovering from the earth a great variety of minerals and mineral products: some are familiar, as with copper and lead; some are relatively unfamiliar, as with columbium or monazite; and some are not always recognized as minerals, as with gems and salt. The techniques and processes of the industries are also far removed from those of the past—though even today they do not always result in ideal conditions for the workers. They involve massive earth-moving equipment, intricate chemical processes, and a host of new automated machines. The work is closer to dam building or construction work than it is to the traditional underground toil of the old-time miner.

There have been parallel changes in the structure of mining companies. As a consequence of the huge amounts of capital involved in excavating, processing, and subsequently transporting minerals on a large scale—to say nothing of the substantial risks and costs of exploring for and developing a deposit—mining activities have inevitably come to be associated with large private or public, national or international firms. Only organizations of this type can raise the capital or generate the funds necessary for modern mining activities, and bear the considerable risks that are inevitably involved.

For example, the initial expense of the Lamco mining project in Liberia, capable of producing 7.5 million tons of iron ore each year, was $200 million. Some 32 percent of this was spent on prospecting, planning, and the construction of the mine itself; nearly 50 percent went into harbor and railroad construction; and a further 10 percent was spent on a township, electricity supply, hospitals, and the like. Subsequently the capacity of the mine was increased to 10 million tons, and a 1.8 million-ton pellet plant was constructed at a cost of about $40 per ton. The increasingly corporate nature of the mining industry, with its headquarters in the largest cities of the world—New York and London, Tokyo and Moscow—has naturally encouraged a growing public interest in their activities. As a consequence, in some circumstances public supervisory agencies and regulatory bodies have been created, while in others governments have assumed all the responsibility for mining activities in their countries. Increasingly affected by decisions taken in the public interest, therefore, the mining industry today must be considered within an appropriate political as well as economic framework.

THE BOOK IN OUTLINE • It is clear that in dealing with so complex and varied an industry in a book as short as this one, only the highlights can be emphasized. These highlights, however, can be treated in such a way as to reveal a great deal that bears not only on the mineral industry but also on the modern economy it supports. For those who wish more detail concerning individual mineral commodities, the list of references at the end of the book affords a suitable springboard into a subject that has a fascinating and burgeoning body of literature.

The next chapter introduces some of the concepts fundamental to an understanding of mineral supply and demand, concepts such as the unique characteristics of the mineral industry's resource base and the problems that these characteristics pose. In Part Two, which comprises the greater part of the book, these characteristics and problems are examined in greater detail as they arise in connection with one or another of the principal mineral commodities. In every case where a specific mineral is discussed, a brief statement following the heading indicates the way in which the mineral is used to illustrate certain characteristics of the mineral industry as a whole. For example, in chapter 3, which deals with the steel industry and iron ore, some indication is given of the changing scale, technology, and complexity of the metal and mineral industries, together with some notion of the shifting patterns of ore supply. Similarly, in the discussion of the alloying elements (chap. 4), the base metals (chap. 5), the light metals (chap. 6), and the industrial minerals and rocks (chap. 7), attention is given to particular themes which sometimes are unique to the mineral in question but more usually have an industry-wide relevance. Thus, in chapter 5 the discussion of copper includes an extended consideration of the meaning of "reserves" and questions related to the measurement of the resource base. The base metals as a whole provide an opportunity to examine the relationship of mineral development to government policy. Lead is used to underline the importance of secondary materials, or scrap, in contemporary mineral supply. The discussion of aluminum in chapter 6 demonstrates the growing importance of substitution in the mineral industry, while the discussion of sulfur and limestone in chapter 7 explores a number of important environmental issues.

Finally, in Part Three the mineral industry is examined as a whole once again. This time emphasis is placed upon the principal determinants of mineral supply in order to provide the reader not only with a better understanding of the past and the present, but also with the means of arriving at reasoned opinions concerning the ways in which minerals might best be used to yield balanced benefits in the future.

2 SOME BASIC CONCEPTS ABOUT MINERALS

MUCH has been written about mineral resources in an attempt to place them in their proper perspective and to answer questions concerning their long-term supply. Such attempts can never be more than partially successful, however, for great uncertainties surround how much mineral wealth actually exists and how much will be used under any given set of conditions. From time to time this uncertainty has given rise to predictions of impending mineral exhaustion, for it is conceivable that at some future date mineral resources may be used up, and at particular places and particular times in the past shortages have, in fact, occurred.

How is it possible to reconcile the concept of increasing use with the concept of limited supply under these uncertain conditions? How reliable are the sources of mineral supply? Where do these growing quantities of materials come from? How can one ensure that supplies are adequate and that they will continue to be so in the future? What are the economics of mineral supply and demand? What are some of the policy considerations entering into the industry's decisions—considerations of security for the firm, the country, or the political-economic bloc, considerations of foreign investment and of aid to developing countries? What about supplies of raw materials for the populations of developing countries as they move towards a standard of living involving greater use of minerals? Are they likely to affect the raw material position of the technologically advanced economies, or not?

These are some of the questions that will be touched upon, rather than answered, in the following pages, for space is limited and in many cases there is no single answer. Much depends upon the assumptions made about technology, economics, and politics, and upon the time and geographical scales that are adopted. The approach and our understanding must vary from mineral to mineral, from user to user, from source to source, and from time to time.

On the fundamental question of the adequacy of mineral supply, however, some concepts do command fairly widespread respect. Since 1952, when the report of the President's Materials Policy Commission (40) was published, the concept that resource availability is largely a matter of cost rather than of finite supplies has been increasingly accepted. There is no evidence that in the relevant past an insufficient supply of minerals has limited economic progress and there is no recorded history of mankind actually running out of a particular mineral. Moreover, it should be made clear at the outset that there is no fundamental shortage of minerals in the world today. Known deposits of a quality that makes them commercially valuable now or in a reasonable time perspective are for most minerals, in fact, greater today than they have ever been. Past shortages have been due to the mineral industry's inability to keep up with sudden surges in demand rather than to any basic lack of natural resources—due, that is, to the inadequacy of man, and not to an inadequacy of raw materials. In recent years changes in ground rules—the passage of health and safety laws, environmental laws, and the introduction of new exploration permit systems, for example—have brought about apparent "shortages." But, while some observers have warned that the world's known reserves of zinc, copper, and lead could be exhausted within the foreseeable future, there are good grounds for taking a less pessimistic view. Later, in chapters 5 and 6, the meaning of such crucial concepts as mineral "reserves" and the importance of such factors as price and substitution are explored to provide an alternative view of medium-term resource availabilities.

What about the more remote future? That the total amount of each and every mineral is fixed and that use diminishes this given stock are inescapable facts. But some counterbalance exists. The availability of minerals is expanded steadily by a growing knowledge of the world's geology, by the falling real costs of transport that allow minerals to be moved over ever-increasing distances, and by the development of techniques that permit the use of different types of ore, often without more costly effort. At the same time, demand is constrained by the discovery of substitutes for some applications, by the development of new ways of doing things that eliminate some uses altogether, and by the improved utilization of the increasing stock of scrap metal. These forces are continually at work, and the pattern of mineral use at any time is the result of their interplay. It is not unreasonable to expect, therefore, that through adjustments involving these and other factors a good balance can be maintained and major problems of mineral inadequacy kept at bay.

The further the time horizon is extended, however, the more this belief must be tempered—if not for all minerals then at least for some —by the consideration that eventually their real costs may begin to rise, and that in a number of applications their use will become uneconomic. Yet this in itself can provide an appropriate mechanism for adjusting demands to the available supplies, since some manufacturers will switch to newly developed substitutes and supply will again be adequate to meet the new demand at the new price.

THE RESOURCE BASE • The earth is the starting point for any discussion of resources. Its crust comprises a variety of minerals, each present in varying percentages in the rocks and soil. Although the amount of any element in a particular rock fragment may be small, the total amount that exists in the earth dwarfs the imagination. If we were to consider the earth as a completely homogeneous mass with the minerals distributed uniformly (following estimates put forward by Professor Kalervo Rankama, of the University of Helsinki), one cubic mile (4.2 cubic kilometers) of rock would contain 1,000 million tons of aluminum, 625 million tons of iron, 260 million tons of magnesium, and over 12 million tons of manganese. These metals are all relatively abundant in the earth's crust. Toward the other end of the scale, a cubic mile of rock would yield over a million tons of zinc, 650,000 tons of copper, 185,000 tons of lead, and even some 60 tons of gold.

But the earth is not homogeneous. Over the hundreds of millions of years a whole chain of geological processes has led to concentrations of particular minerals or groups of minerals in certain areas in percentages that are far higher than the average for the crust. If the United States were to get its requirements of iron from a homogeneous crust, it would be necessary to excavate a quarry 100 feet (30 meters) deep and 5 to 6 square miles (8 to 10 square kilometers) in area each year. Instead, the ore is up to ten times as rich, and so, allowing for differences in density, the quarry would have to cover slightly more than half a square mile. Copper concentration in some ores may be 1,000 times greater than the crustal average, lead ore 3,000 times greater. Where possible, the mineral industry recovers its material from these highly enriched zones found irregularly throughout the world. But these random concentrations are frequently hard to locate and develop.

It might be asked why it is not possible to take from reasonably average rock not only iron but also all other needed mineral materials as they are required. This would involve putting rock in at one end of a plant, breaking it down into its component parts, and meeting most mineral needs in one complex production operation. It is an intriguing idea and one that is by no means completely unreasonable, although a great deal of research and experimentation would be required to put it into practice. A few years ago, Professor Harrison Brown of the California Institute of Technology expressed the belief that mineral requirements will one day be so great that all significant concentrations of minerals—everything that is classed today as a mineral deposit—will be used up, but a highly developed world will continue to prosper, using raw materials obtained by breaking down common rocks such as granite. Iron, aluminum, sulfur, phosphorus, and all the other elements contained in rocks will provide the mineral materials we need. Uranium and other radioactive elements will provide the power to process the rock and to run the world. (5, pp. 216–17)

So far it has not been necessary or economical to develop such a system as this, but there is a perceptible movement toward it in today's use of lower-grade materials, and in the recovery of progressively more of the usable materials in the ores that are mined. Perhaps some day mineral needs will be met from common rock. If one considers this as even a remote possibility, then mineral supply is constrained only by the limits of the earth's crust—or at least those portions of it that are accessible to man without undue consumption of other resources.

In considering mineral supply in the purely physical sense then, adequacy for the indefinite future may well be an appropriate view. Most of this material is far too costly to develop today, and it may never be worth developing in the future. However, so long as we have not dug up the backyard to extract the clay to produce aluminum, nor ground up the rocks in the neighboring park to recover their minor content of copper or iron, we have not run out of mineral-bearing material. Long before man is reduced to this, of course, these metals will have become sufficiently costly to restrict them to only a few applications in which they cannot be replaced.

These, then, are some of the basic terms of reference within which to consider the questions that have been posed on world mineral supply. The physical or geological environment from which we get our minerals in the future may be quite different from that of today. The processes by which minerals are recovered also may be quite different; the emphasis on particular minerals may shift. When the question of adequate mineral resources is considered within this extraordinarily large framework of the "resource base" (or the "total stock" as it is sometimes called), then it is not unreasonable to believe that the more extreme limits to physical supply will always remain a distant horizon.

THE COMMODITIES • How do we subdivide the mineral world? There are many possible approaches. A geologist would be quick to point out that most of the rocks of the world are made up of minerals such as quartz, calcite, feldspar, biotite, hornblende, and a variety of other so-called rock-forming minerals, many of which contain aluminum, iron, magnesium, and traces of other metals, but not in a form useful to today's miners. Except as they may fall into the group of industrial rocks—quartz is the only mineral component of glass sand, and calcium carbonate ($CaCo_3$) the only mineral component of limestone— we are not concerned with these rock-forming minerals. Rather, we are interested in what the geologist terms "economic minerals," or minerals used by man. Each such mineral is, on the one hand, a part of a rock that contains a mixture of minerals and, on the other hand, a chemical compound containing within it certain metals and other elements.

These minerals can be classified in a number of ways, one of which divides the mineral world into three major groups: the mineral fuels, the metallic minerals, and the nonmetallic minerals (also referred to as industrial minerals and rocks), on the basis of a combination of their use and their physical and chemical characteristics.

As can be seen in table 1, in the United States in 1970 the mineral fuels (coal, petroleum, and natural gas) are far and away the largest sector, accounting for over two-thirds of the value of mineral production. The same is true on a global basis. Although this group shares many characteristics with the metallic and nonmetallic minerals, it is usually treated separately. This is partly because it is so large, complex, and important that it would tend to overshadow any other branch of the mineral industry with which it was included. For this reason, and also because one volume cannot hope to deal in a balanced way with the whole range of mineral raw materials, this book is confined to a discussion of the metallic and the nonmetallic minerals (for brevity usually termed metals and nonmetals) and refers to the mineral fuels only occasionally where they are related to these two groups.

There is also a logical split between metals and nonmetals which, as the terms themselves indicate, is based upon the physical characteristics of the two groups. But there are other differences. The metals, by and large, occur in combination with other elements from which they must be separated. The nonmetals are used in much the same form in which they are mined and require relatively little process-

TABLE 1

Value of U.S. mineral production, 1970	Mineral Fuels	$20,153,000
	Nonmetallic minerals	5,710,815
	Metallic minerals	3,926,000
	Total	$29,790,000

Source: U.S. Bureau of Mines (10, pp. 106, 107).

ing. Whereas metals are relatively high in price, much of the total value of nonmetallic minerals comes from the production of such low-priced materials as limestone, sand, gravel, and clay, which occur in relative abundance and are produced mainly for local consumption. Thus, while metals are international commodities, most nonmetals rarely enter into world trade. There are important exceptions, of course— diamonds and asbestos being two examples.

Figure 1 shows the way the major metals and nonmetals are commonly subdivided. In dealing with the metals, consideration will be given to the first four major categories and some of the metals included in each. Two metals—gold and silver—that are internationally prominent in many ways are not dealt with at all since their role in the monetary field endows them with many special aspects that are unrepresentative of metals in general. In the case of the nonmetals, the treatment is more general. It nevertheless touches upon the principal characteristics of the group, using sulfur and limestone as examples.

THE COMPLEXITY OF MINERAL SUPPLY • A discussion of the metals and nonmetals still leaves a good deal of territory to be investigated, for each material has its own complex features and problems. For example, consider the factors involved in developing a new source of mineral supply by bringing a new metal mine into production. To warrant development (in a market or mixed economy), a deposit must have a size, grade, and location that allows it to be mined at a profit. The search is for those few deposits that meet these conditions and— since past prospecting has found the ones that can be easily located— the search must be ingenious, making use of every scientific tool available to find deposits that have remained undiscovered. They may be buried by layers of rock, in which case geophysical or geochemical methods which detect evidences of buried deposits are employed. They may be hidden in the remote corners of the earth, in which case the problems are not only those of finding the deposits, but also those of getting men and equipment to the site to develop them.

Discovery is, of course, only the first step. Once the mineral deposit has been located, technical decisions must be made on the way in which the deposit should be developed. Economic decisions are needed on whether such development can be financed and is likely to yield an acceptable rate of return. Political decisions are required on the terms under which mineral operations can be undertaken. It is normal to think of political decisions in connection with foreign development, but they are also important in a domestic context, most commonly in the case of construction materials, such as sand and gravel, which are developed in areas of high population. In the case of a fully planned economy, such as that of the U.S.S.R.,

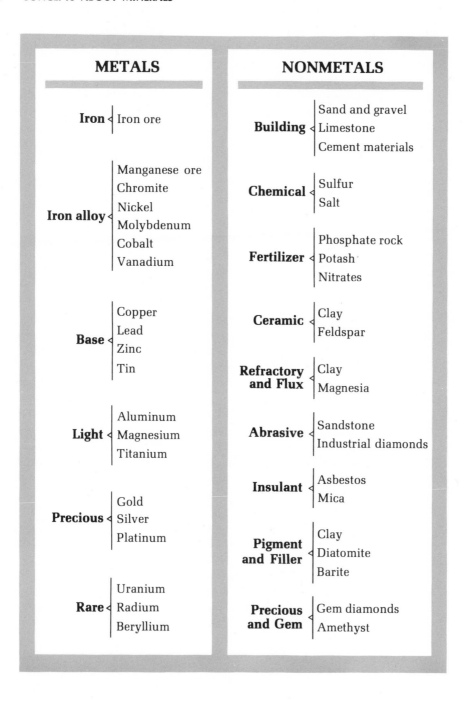

METALS

Iron ⟨ Iron ore

Iron alloy ⟨ Manganese ore
Chromite
Nickel
Molybdenum
Cobalt
Vanadium

Base ⟨ Copper
Lead
Zinc
Tin

Light ⟨ Aluminum
Magnesium
Titanium

Precious ⟨ Gold
Silver
Platinum

Rare ⟨ Uranium
Radium
Beryllium

NONMETALS

Building ⟨ Sand and gravel
Limestone
Cement materials

Chemical ⟨ Sulfur
Salt

Fertilizer ⟨ Phosphate rock
Potash
Nitrates

Ceramic ⟨ Clay
Feldspar

Refractory and Flux ⟨ Clay
Magnesia

Abrasive ⟨ Sandstone
Industrial diamonds

Insulant ⟨ Asbestos
Mica

Pigment and Filler ⟨ Clay
Diatomite
Barite

Precious and Gem ⟨ Gem diamonds
Amethyst

Figure 1. How metals and nonmetals are commonly grouped.

politico-economic objectives play a decisive part in shaping the pattern of mineral resource exploitation, and these may outweigh the more purely commercial considerations.

After the key decision to utilize a resource, there follows the period of development, which often includes building roads, railroads, port facilities, power stations, and complete communities. Only after all this has been done is there any actual production. Even then, the product of the mine is nothing more than a rock relatively rich in mineral; it may contain 5 tons of copper in 1,000 tons of rock—one hundred times the amount in the average crust, but still just a rock to anyone unfamiliar with copper ore.

Somewhere along its journey from mine to market the mineral, if it is a metallic ore, must be concentrated, smelted, refined, and converted into relatively pure metal. Even then it is not ready for use. It must be rolled, drawn, or otherwise changed into forms usable by the fabricators and manufacturers who make the final consumer products.

The operations involved in these processes are well illustrated by the copper development at Toquepala, in southern Peru. In developing this mining area, the participating companies, largely American, had to locate the property; the first options were taken in 1937. After this they had to negotiate local leases and terms of operation, and raise the capital for development (including a $100 million loan from the Export-Import Bank of the United States). Only then, by about 1954, were they ready to develop the mine. The mine workings, the crushing plant, the concentrator, the waste disposal area, the workshops—all these one would expect. But in addition the developers had to find people with the necessary skills who would live in this area, and build for them a mine townsite that could accommodate over 3,700 employees and their families, complete with hospitals, schools, and recreational facilities. At Toquepala, high in the mountains of southern Peru, the mine produces ore and the processing plant adjacent to the mine produces the copper concentrate. To move this concentrate it was necessary to build 110 miles (176 kilometers) of railroad to the coast. At the coast, a second townsite, Ilo, was built, with a smelter to produce blister copper (a rough copper metal), and a pier capable of accommodating deep-draft ocean vessels. The whole operation had to be supplied with power and water. The total initial cost: some $250 million.

This mine began production in January 1960, and soon blister copper, plus a molybdenum concentrate by-product, was moving from Peru to world markets in important quantities—nearly 130,000 tons each year at the end of that decade. The exported blister copper is not, of course, the final copper product. It must be further refined at plants in the United States and Western Europe before it is sold to fabricators to be made into sheets and rods and wire which can be used by manufacturers.

In 1969 contracts were signed with the Peruvian government for the development of the nearby Cuajone deposits at an additional cost of $418 million. The current attitude of the Peruvian government toward foreign investment is by no means clear, however. In 1973 it began action to repurchase some of these foreign-held copper operations. While the mining companies view the action as confiscatory at the price offered, the government claims it is justified by the failure of the companies to live up to their social expenditure commitments. Conflicts in the interests of mining companies and host countries are an inherent risk in establishing major mineral operations in developing countries, and these risks weigh heavily in foreign investment decisions.

Although the story of the development of the copper mining and smelting industry in southern Peru is still unfolding, its initial stages indicate some of the ways in which the problems of supplying minerals can be categorized: into the exploration, development, production, processing, and fabricating stages; and into technical, economic, political, and social considerations. This book touches upon as many of these aspects as possible. It goes beyond a simple description of the sources of supply and the statistics on world production and consumption, to deal with some of the reasons for mineral supply patterns, and especially some of the economic, political, and social factors that affect them.

THE GEOGRAPHY OF SUPPLY • One fundamental and unique characteristic of mineral deposits sets mineral raw materials apart from other forms of raw material used in both primitive and technologically advanced economies. This is the "fixed" nature of mineral deposits—the fact that they are fixed in location, fixed in size, and fixed in their physical and chemical properties. The key variables in mineral development, then, are to be found in the socioeconomic and political environment which makes use of the minerals; and critical elements of this environment include the level of need and the type of technology that can be directed to meet this need. Fixed location—and the fact that mineral deposits are unequally distributed through the crust of the earth—when combined with fixed quantity—which means that individual mineral deposits can be used up—leads to some of the more challenging problems of the mineral industry.

Nickel from Canada, mercury from Spain, graphite from the Malagasy Republic, mica from India—these are all part of the traditional pattern by which minerals have been supplied to world industry. The pattern is more complex and inflexible than that for other types of raw materials because of the fixed nature of mineral deposits. At present, two of the world's most important deposits of nickel have been mined from the ancient Precambrian rocks of Ontario and Manitoba in Canada. The most important deposits of molybdenum have been discovered in the eastern margin of the North American Cordillera where, around Climax, Colorado, at least half the world's production has been mined over the past fifty years. Some of the world's major reserves of manganese are in the U.S.S.R.; tungsten, in China; cobalt, in the Republic of Zaire. A narrow belt running from southern China through Thailand, Malaysia, and Indonesia produces the bulk of the world's tin. These are perhaps extreme examples, but by no means the only ones. Toward the other end of the scale, some minerals are much more widespread and abundant; a few examples are the deposits of iron ore and coal that spawned some of the world's great industrial regions, and the salt and clay that are readily available in many parts of the globe.

The distinctive geography of many mineral resources, however, does pose some inescapable problems. A dispersion of sources throughout the world is not a pattern that either a corporate or a national component of the mineral industry would naturally choose for its raw material supply. It is a costly pattern to establish and maintain, and is at the mercy of a wide variety of people and governments. Prices may be controlled by a few producers to the disadvantage of mineral users in general. Local strikes may temporarily withhold supplies, while both short-term and more permanent interruptions of supplies can follow the actions of national governments.

Minerals have been used in the past as weapons in economic warfare, as for example when the U.S.S.R. abruptly cut off exports of manganese to the United States in late 1948. Large users of mineral raw materials, such as the United States, Western Europe, and Japan, would naturally prefer to be less vulnerable in so important an area of their economies. For many producers and industrial countries, minerals are not only fixed in location, they are often fixed in undesirable locations.

Is industry committed to this pattern? Not completely, for over a period of time there is a remarkable degree of flexibility in the sources of mineral supply. The actual flow of mineral raw materials in world trade is dictated partly by economics, partly by the inertia of traditional relationships, and partly by a variety of other factors among which international politics is prominent. The result is quite different from what it would be if the economic characteristics of the deposit were the only controlling factor and access to the reserves of the world were completely free. Since the Russian revolution, for example, the U.S.S.R. has placed a very high premium upon acquiring and maintaining a high level of self-sufficiency in mineral raw materials, and there can be no doubt that its present pattern of mineral use and trade would not pertain in a market economy.

Similarly, although the U.S.S.R. has major reserves of manganese and is the world's largest producer, it still does not export to the United States, which has come to rely upon a variety of alternative sources, expecially Brazil and Gabon. Following the interruption of Soviet supplies in the late 1940s, the United States substituted other minerals in some applications, carried out technical research to reduce consumption, and assisted in the opening up of new deposits of manganese in several parts of the world. In all probability these known deposits are not the only major sources of manganese in the earth. Politics change; mineral supply patterns change also.

Historically, man-made political boundaries have helped to shape mineral development, and mineral deposits have affected politics. The border between France and Germany for many years was in dispute not least of all because it lies adjacent to the low-grade but plentiful iron ore deposits of Lorraine, and the development of that resource has been in considerable measure a function of the changing relationship between the two countries as well as the complementary mineral endowments of the nearby Ruhr. The richest copper belt in the world, in Central Africa, is cut by the border between Zambia and the Katanga Province of Zaire, countries with somewhat contrasting political histories and hence mineral development strategies. The U.S.S.R., in remaking its boundaries with Finland after World War II, was careful to embrace the nickel deposits of Petsamo and thus to commit those resources to a pattern of exploitation within the framework of a fully planned economy.

To the extent that political boundaries and international relationships have demonstrably affected patterns of mineral development and supply in the past, contemporary and future political decisions can continue to influence the behavior of the industry. Only in 1960 did the government of the Commonwealth of Australia give permission for exploration and development of iron ore resources in Western Australia for export markets. Within a decade output had increased tenfold, and from a position of relative insignificance the country was on the way to becoming the third largest producer of that mineral in the world, after the U.S.S.R. and the United States.

Technological changes can also alter mineral supply patterns. Although mineral deposits are fixed, the characteristics that make a particular mineral concentration economic are not. New techniques can make a material usable. There may be ways of using low-grade, formerly waste, material or of using new source rocks hitherto considered unacceptable. For many decades the iron and steel industry of the United States relied upon the famous direct-shipping ores of the Lake Superior region to feed most of its blast furnaces; but in recent years these mines have been phased out of production as new technology and economics have made the pellets produced from taconite economically more attractive. Future supplies of aluminum ores could well be affected by similar kinds of technological development. The principal source of aluminum today is bauxite, found mainly in the tropics. However, clay, which occurs commonly throughout the world, is a rich potential source of aluminum, and research is in progress to develop a suitable method for recovering aluminum from it. A breakthrough here would completely change the mineral supply pattern for aluminum production in the United States, for example, since clay deposits, abundant in America, could replace bauxite imports.

Another way in which technology is contributing to future mineral supplies is through the development of tools and techniques to locate as yet undiscovered deposits. Many of the best mineral deposits, it is believed, lie hidden at some depth beneath the surface. Over the years, scientists, particularly geophysicists and geochemists, have been able to learn much about the subsurface. Geophysical techniques have been spectacularly successful in locating oil, and modern petroleum exploration is preceded by detailed seismic surveys. Similar techniques are used in locating metals and nonmetals. Airborne electromagnetometers found the nickel deposits developed at Thompson Lake in Manitoba; seismic surveys are used to locate salt and sulfur in the Gulf Coast area; resistivity surveys helped to find lead-zinc deposits in New Brunswick; a gravity survey located a barite deposit on one of the islands of Greece. These techniques are being continually refined to give more precise readings and to probe deeper beneath the crust—including, of course, the crust beneath the seas, on which nodules rich in manganese, cobalt, and nickel could in time come to serve man's needs (see chap. 4).

Geochemical exploration, involving systematic testing of the metal content of rocks or soil in an area, or of the leaves and branches of certain trees, can give useful information on buried mineral deposits. Mineral concentrations emit a sort of halo which spreads well beyond the area in which they are located, and geochemical testing can help to detect them. In the United States this relatively inexpensive technique has helped to locate deposits of such minerals as copper, lead, zinc, uranium, and cobalt, and in the Soviet Union it has been applied over very wide areas in conjunction with other exploration methods.

Another way in which mineral supply patterns can become more flexible lies in the improvement and declining real costs of transport. Over the past two decades modern technology and organization of ocean transport together have for the first time permitted bulk mineral supplies to be moved economically and on a regular basis halfway round the world. From West Africa to Japan and Australia to Britain, minerals are now being shipped at freight rates considerably lower than those charged twenty years ago. Very large bulk carriers of 80,000 deadweight tons and more, chartered on a long-term contract and often indirectly subsidized, today enable raw materials, particularly iron ore and bauxite, to bear the costs of a sea journey covering some 11,000 nautical miles and still compete with more traditional sources of ore one-hundredth of the distance away. Improvements in ocean transport have been paralleled, but not matched, by advancing technology and lower costs in railroad transport and even in road haulage; and all three have been supplemented in some special instances by the use of the pipeline.

Patterns of mineral supply, therefore, do change; and they can be made to change. The deserts of Chile were formerly the world's major source of nitrates. But Germany, cut off from Chilean nitrates during World War I, succeeded in evolving processes for the recovery of nitrogen from coal and from the atmosphere. These processes have ended the world's reliance on naturally occurring material. Likewise, at one time the world depended upon Sicily for its sulfur, but the discovery of sulfur-bearing salt domes in the Gulf Coast region of the United States completely transformed the traditional pattern. For over sixty years this new source virtually dominated the world industry. By the early 1950s, however, demand began to outstrip supply, prices hardened, and scarcity seemed imminent. Again the situation was reversed almost overnight with the rapid expansion of Canadian natural gas production, which happens to be "sour" and a rich source of sulfur. By 1972 the output of this "recovered" sulfur was approaching the production level of "Frasch" sulfur from the Gulf Coast. And a final example: the republics of Zaire and South Africa still control the diamond supply of the world, but this is threatened on the one hand by rich new discoveries in Siberia, and on the other by the rapidly improving techniques for producing synthetic diamonds.

Thus it would appear that although mineral deposits are fixed in location, a series of mechanisms exists to make this rigidity a relative rather than an absolute characteristic. There are far more deposits than was once thought, and the range of usable material is broader than it was even a few years ago. Rich deposits of most minerals are undoubtedly still awaiting discovery and development. In addition, there are many known deposits in a lower order of exploitability. Some of these are being worked today but are not large enough to be leaders in world supply; others could be operated economically if the price of their raw material were to be a little higher, or if markets were assured by such devices as bilateral trade agreements or a corporate take-over.

Thus, although it must be true in the absolute physical sense that minerals are fixed in location and fixed in amount, the part of the "total stock" that is known to man or that can be used by man is by no means fixed. It is one of the paradoxes of the mineral industry that as more minerals are used more seem to be available for further use. A partial explanation for this phenomenon may be found in the way in which the mineral industry tends to evaluate its medium-term reserves. The costs of exploration are very high and the risks considerable. It follows, therefore, that there is little incentive for any mining concern to prove the existence of a reserve if the likelihood of its use in the next twenty years is quite small. Future mineral wealth discounted back to present values has a remarkably small book value. With longer-term mineral reserves discounted by the mining industry in this way, at least in a market economy, it is inevitable that knowledge concerning the true size of a country's mineral wealth is much scantier than is generally realized—even in countries as advanced technologically as the United States and Australia. (In a fully planned economy, by contrast, the costs and risks of mineral exploration are carried by the state and not the individual mining and metal industries; as a consequence, and also as a matter of policy, there is sometimes a tendency to prove the existence of reserves irrespective of immediate needs.) Current reserves, then, tend to be basically a fifteen- to twenty-year working inventory of a mineral resource which is adjusted upwards as needs require; they are by no means a complete statement of the mineral wealth available in the ground. It is not surprising, in this context, that major new discoveries of minerals continue to be made and that the reserves of particular metals and nonmetallic raw materials are constantly revised upwards. We return to these points in chapter 5.

Such a situation is also highly dependent upon a continually improving technology in developing low-grade materials and substitutes, and in time this may lead to higher prices. At that point, for certain applications the use of these materials would cease to be economical. In this connection, however, it is interesting to look at what has happened to copper. The conventional argument goes something like this: As minerals are used, the rich deposits become depleted and copper becomes more expensive to mine; as industry costs go up, the price of metal must go up in order to encourage the production of the necessary amounts of copper; as the price rises, it becomes economical to use more abundant materials of lower metallic content, and new reserves are created; these in turn will be mined and depleted. The cycle can go on and on and can never really end, for as the mineral material becomes progressively more costly to produce, substitutes enter and take over some of the market, some users drop out, others use their material more efficiently, scrap recovery improves, and at the same time as ore grade decreases, the quantities available continue to increase. There is, however, a question as to the inevitability of rising prices. According to a study of copper's price behavior made by Resources for the Future a few years ago (20), this unattractive feature of the cycle has been missing over the past eighty years. It seems that technology has kept pace, and savings due to more efficient methods of development and recovery have been sufficient to offset factors that would have made for cost increases. A more recent RFF study on the future supplies of the major metals (26) indicates that by and large the same may hold true in the foreseeable future for other metals.

For practical purposes, therefore, it is important to recognize that the usable volume and variety of minerals increase as technology advances. Just as over the centuries mankind has learned to use a host of materials of no previous value or of only a limited value, so it is reasonable to expect that in the future mineral supplies and demands will steadily change. At a more immediate and local level individual deposits do, of course, become exhausted, presenting very real problems to mining companies and miners. In order to keep up its reserves, the company must find a new ore body while the old deposit is being worked out; and the miner, whether he likes it or not, must be a mobile individual.

Usually, however, it is not so much a matter of the mineral reserves actually running out as of the ore grade steadily decreasing and mining costs gradually increasing so that an operation becomes uneconomic. This accounts for the fact that many mines have operated intermittently over centuries with long periods of inactivity. From time to time man makes a technological breakthrough, which changes the conditions under which mines can be profitably operated and allows old mines to be reopened. The Greeks took the rich silver ores from Laurium near Athens 2,000 years ago, paying relatively little attention to the large amounts of lead that accompanied the silver. During this century a French company went back into the area and was able to mine the remaining lead ores at a profit. In recent years renewed interest has been aroused in Britain's historical nonferrous mining areas of Cornwall and Snowdonia. Indeed, today many almost forgotten mining districts are among the most attractive areas for new development, for it is known that they still contain mineral wealth, and in many cases modern techniques permit the extraction of that wealth at a profit.

In the United States, the iron ore situation is perhaps the best illustration of the way in which the prophets of doom have been confounded about the problems of fixed quantity. The country has been about to run out of iron ore time and time again. The early furnaces of Pennsylvania were based on hundreds of small lenses of iron ore in the local mountains. As each deposit was exhausted the furnace it fed closed down. Today the state is blanketed with villages bearing names ending in "Forge" or "Furnace," of which Valley Forge is probably the best known. This pattern gradually changed as rich ores from the Lake Superior district were discovered and developed. These became the principal source of iron ore for U.S. industry, supplying over 80 percent of requirements during most of this century. The Second World War was supposed to have dealt the death blow to Lake Superior mining, for the best ore was gouged from the earth at an unprecedented rate, and in the postwar period there was a scramble for new overseas sources—in Labrador, in Venezuela, in Africa—to replace the dying Mesabi. But today the Lake Superior district continues as a major source of ore for the United States' iron and steel industry and is known to contain far greater riches than once was thought—almost limitless quantities of low-grade taconites. As in the case of copper, the base of available material has been expanded with no significant increase of cost.

TWO · COMMODITY STUDIES: in

 which a number of the major mineral raw materials are used to illustrate various aspects and issues of mineral supply and development

3 THE STEEL INDUSTRY AND IRON ORE: in which some indication is given of the complexity of the mineral industry as it relates to a key metal– the many materials which must be acquired and assembled–the many places from which they come–the changes in these patterns of supply

STEEL remains the most important metal and one of the most vital industrial raw materials of modern society. It is not a metal in the sense that copper or lead is. The pure metal is iron, but iron does not possess enough strength and hardness to make it of great use to industry. It is treated, therefore, with other elements to improve its qualities. Basic steel is, in fact, iron to which a small amount of carbon (usually only a fraction of 1 percent) has been added. This is the recipe on which world industry is based.

Iron has been known and used for a long time, and even steel is not a new discovery. The art of steelmaking has been found, lost, and rediscovered many times and in many places—China, India, Spain —and each time it was highly prized. In the twen-

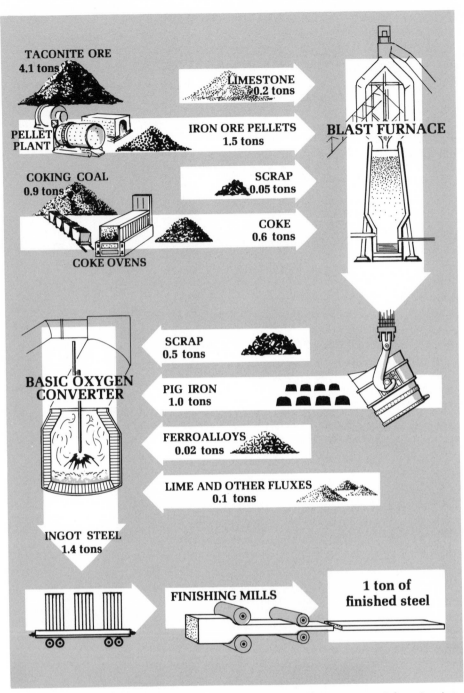

Figure 2. Ingredients for a ton of finished steel. The raw materials going into pig iron, plus other ingredients used in steelmaking, add up to over 5 tons. In addition, substantial quantities of water, fuel oil, electricity, oxygen, and refractories are used.

tieth century, cheap, reliable methods of making steel have been fundamental to the development of industrial technology and have made possible a rising level of material development in many parts of the world.

Compared with all other metal industries, steel is the giant, dwarfing the rest. Over 90 percent of the metal produced in the world each year is steel; and steel is mainly iron. Many of the other metals—nickel, chromium, manganese—are not essential in their own right. They are produced mainly to be added to the steel mix to give it special qualities. The steel industry is so large because its product is exceptionally versatile and has many uses; its raw materials are abundant and relatively easy to assemble and process; and the resulting material is cheap. Carbon steel—and most steel is plain carbon steel—costs less than 8 cents a pound (17½ cents a kilogram) in the United States. In refrigerators, automobiles, and the wide variety of consumer goods that are made of steel the metal makes up the greater part of the product but accounts for only a small fraction of the cost.

The steel industry is so complex and has interests in so many parts of the world and sectors of the mineral industry that it would be quite possible to draw from it all of our examples of minerals operations and problems. But in order to broaden our outlook we shall not do this; rather, the steel industry will be used to show something of the shifting framework within which the metal and mineral industries operate—the changing technological complexity, the constant movement in the location of mineral demands, the reevaluation of geographical space and distance with the use of modern transport facilities, and other factors that bear upon new patterns of mineral supply, including the politico-economic issue of self-sufficiency. All these it illustrates excellently.

THE PROCESSES • Man seldom finds metals in a form that can be used. He finds rock which contains metal, and he must devise ways to extract this material economically. Sometimes this is relatively simple, sometimes very difficult. The details can be omitted, but the methods used to make so important a product as steel do deserve some attention. Here iron ore is the rock. It contains iron, which is required, along with a number of impurities which must be removed. The oxide, iron ore, is heated with a carbon fuel; gas is released when the carbon in the fuel combines with the oxygen in the iron ore; and metallic iron is left as a residue.

The basic process, shown in figure 2, is simple. It could be imitated by heating a piece of iron ore under draught in a charcoal fire. Here, the result would be a lump of spongy iron which, with hammering and reheating, could be shaped into an axe or a spade or some other useful tool or implement. Processes little more advanced than this are still used by primitive societies.

Modern technology is more sophisticated and more economical, but still carbon is made to combine with the oxygen in iron ore, thereby releasing metallic iron for further processing. The ores of iron, in terms of their iron content, their chemistry, and their physical structure, exhibit a considerable variety. The cheapest to reduce to pig iron are generally the magnetites (Fe_3O_4) and the hematites (Fe_2O_3), which contain rather less than 70 percent iron. Limonites ($2Fe_2O_3 \cdot 3H_2O$) and siderites ($FeCo_3$) are also reduced in some parts of the world.

At one time most ores were fed directly into the blast furnace, but increasingly it has been found advantageous to beneficiate and agglomerate many of them in such a way as to increase their iron content and also make their physical and chemical properties more consistent. Simple crushing and grading has given way to sintering and pelletizing until today over 90 percent of all the ore produced in the United States is beneficiated in some way, adding considerably to the value of the ore. Mined in an open pit, the cost of ore including taxes and royalties might be in the order of $5 per ton; made into pellets the value per ton more than doubles.

The carbon needed to combine with oxygen in the ore is provided in the form of coke, i.e., bituminous coal from which most components other than carbon and a small residue of irreducible ash have been eliminated. Coke is a vital part of the steelmaking process and the coke ovens of the steel industry are one of the largest single markets for bituminous coal—just under 79 million tons in the United States in 1970. Sometimes, in the most modern furnaces, the coke is supplemented with natural gas or fuel oil in order to increase the temperature and improve its performance. A final major raw material is limestone, which combines with impurities in the iron ore to form slag. Some of the largest limestone quarries in the world serve the steel companies, which, again in the United States in 1970, used nearly 21 million tons in the production of 84 million tons of pig iron.

The Blast Furnace. Most iron ore is reduced to metallic iron in blast furnaces—great cylindrical steel towers, over 200 feet (60 meters) high, lined with refractories and having a hearth diameter of up to 36 feet (11 meters). Their daily output lies in the range of 3,000 to 5,000 tons per day, using a high-quality feed, although one Japanese furnace has produced over 10,000 tons in a 24-hour period. There are other processes for reducing ore, but none that has been able to compete in cost and efficiency with the coke-fueled blast furnace for large-scale production.

Coke is the key to the success of the blast furnace process. It provides the major part of the heat needed to melt the ore. It also provides the carbon which serves as a reducing agent to combine with and remove the oxygen. Because it is a strong, porous, chunky material, retaining its shape even when almost consumed, a central column of partially burned coke is capable of supporting the weight of hundreds of tons of charge pressing down toward the base of the blast furnace. Before coke came into common use a hundred years ago, charcoal, a weaker fuel, was used; the early blast furnaces were therefore low and had only a small capacity.

The basic raw materials—iron ore, coke, and limestone—are charged into the top of the furnace and gradually work their way down through progressively hotter zones. A blast of hot air, in recent years often enriched with oxygen, is blown into the furnace through openings called tuyeres near the bottom. The oxygen enables the coke to burn and also reacts with some of the carbon from the coke to form carbon monoxide. This in turn reacts with the iron ore to produce metallic iron and carbon dioxide, building up intense heat in the process. The molten metallic iron so formed collects at the bottom of the furnace.

Iron ore contains a good deal of earthy impurity which also goes into the furnace and which must be removed. This is accomplished by the limestone in the original charge. Converted into lime in the intense heat, the limestone helps to form a liquid slag containing most of these impurities, which drips down to float on top of the heavier iron.

The iron, now "pig iron," is tapped off at the base of the furnace every five or six hours in casts of 300 tons or more, and moves on to further processing. The slag is tapped more often and carried away to the slag dumps, basically as a waste product. Industry, however, can use much of this slag—some in place of gravel or crushed rock in making concrete, some for processing into mineral wool insulation. The gases produced in the blast furnace are cleaned and recycled, providing heat at other parts of the steel plant or nearby industry.

Blast furnace operation is continuous. Iron ore, coke, and limestone continue to be fed into the top, to work their way down through the furnace at about 15 feet (5 meters) per hour, and to emerge as pig iron and slag at the bottom. Periodically, perhaps once every four or five years, the blast furnace is closed down so that its refractory brick lining can be repaired, a process that might take as long as three months.

Linings for a modern blast furnace and its auxiliary units may require over 3 million special bricks which may be made from silica, clay, magnesite, or chromite, depending on their purpose. The bricks must be able to withstand the high temperatures within the furnace, the erosion of the charge as it works its way down through the furnace, and the corrosive action of the gases generated in the process;

they must also conserve the heat in the furnace to keep the fuel costs down. Refractory bricks perform these vital functions both in steel-making and in the processing of most other metals.

Steelmaking. The blast furnace produces pig iron, a metal which is about 90 to 95 percent iron, but still contains up to 4 percent carbon, 1 percent manganese, and minor amounts of silicon, sulfur, and phosphorus as impurities. Some pig iron is used directly in foundries to make cast iron articles; but in general pig iron has relatively few uses, for it is hard and brittle, and so needs further processing.

Most of the pig iron is transferred, still molten, to be further purified in one of several types of furnace. It is widely accepted that the most economical type today is the basic oxygen converter (27, p. 47). This is an adaptation of the earlier and relatively simple Bessemer process in which molten pig iron is placed in a pear-shaped vessel and hot air is blown in from the bottom, generating a considerable amount of heat (steelmaking temperatures are in the region of 3,000°F, or 1,650°C), and causing the silicon, manganese, and carbon in the metal to oxidize. In the basic oxygen converter, on the other hand, an oxygen lance is lowered into the top of the vessel and large quantities of oxygen are blown in at supersonic speeds. Computer controlled, this process affords a flexible and speedy method of making steel: vessels ranging from 50 to 300 tons in capacity can complete their cycle of being charged, making steel, and being emptied in a mere thirty to forty minutes. Pig iron is only one part of the charge: steel scrap, which on average makes up between 35 and 45 percent of the charge, depending upon its price and availability, is also especially important; and limestone, plus other fluxes, are added to form a slag and to remove impurities.

The final characteristics of steel are determined in the converter. Some 90 percent of all steel produced is poured directly into molds of 5 to 25 ton capacity to solidify as ingots. This is carbon steel. The remaining 10 percent is special-purpose steel, to which must be added precise amounts of alloying elements such as chromium, nickel, or tungsten, which can greatly change its properties. Supplying these materials is another important industry on which many people in distant parts of the world depend (see chap. 4).

Twenty years ago, the most common method of making steel was in the open-hearth furnace, which is still to be found in many steel-making centers today. These furnaces are shallow basins or hearths about 100 feet (30 meters) long and 25 feet wide, which contain a shallow pool of molten metal between approximately 26 and 30 inches (65 and 75 centimeters) deep. Again, pig iron is only part of the charge. Iron ore, which may make up 2 to 20 percent of the charge and which is used to provide a source of oxygen to combine with the excess carbon, is added along with the pig iron, limestone, and scrap. Sweeping flames of hot air and gas, oil, pitch, or tar are then played over the charge. The whole process, which takes about eight to ten hours, is under constant survey so that the composition of the melt can be carefully controlled; once the melt is finished, the steel is tapped into a giant ladle. Steel is also made in electric arc furnaces, in which scrap metal is the main raw material. This process is well adapted to making special-purpose steels, for the degree of quality control is particularly accurate.

Scrap is an important source of many metals and will be dealt with in some detail in the discussion of lead in chapter 5. In the making of steel it is not only a substitute for newly mined metal, but an important raw material in its own right. The total metallic input for steel made in the United States is normally 51 to 53 percent pig iron, 42 to 44 percent scrap, with the balance made up of ferroalloys and, in the case of open-hearth furnaces, iron ore.

Much of the scrap is generated from within the industry itself. Thus, for example, when a steel mill gets an order for 100 tons of sheet steel, it actually produces about 140 tons of steel ingots of required grade. After these ingots have gone through the soaking pit and have been rolled into a slab in a mill, some 35 tons of relatively poor-quality steel are cropped off the ends of the slab and recycled as scrap. Through the whole steelmaking process similar croppings and trimmings accumulate and are reused as so-called "home" or "works" scrap. Additional scrap is also available from engineering and manufacturing plants in which steel is used, and is known as "process" or "prompt industrial" scrap. The steel industry can also make use of old automobile frames and other used iron and steel products—scrap as we normally think of it. This is "capital" or "obsolete" scrap, and it is used in varying quantities depending on its price, quality, and availability.

The iron and steel industry is characterized by the vast quantities of materials that must be found and assembled for its use (figure 2). In the United States, which still has the largest national production of steel in the world—an output of 119 million tons in 1970, compared with 116 million in the U.S.S.R., 93 million in Japan, and 45 million in West Germany (table 2)—an enormous volume of materials is assembled each year. To make that 119 million tons of steel in 1970, the industry used 130 million tons of iron ore, 84 million tons of coal for making coke and raising steam, 23 million tons of limestone, 66 million tons of scrap metal, and over 1 million tons of alloying elements. The list could go on. For example, in 1970 the steel industry consumed about 1,200 million U.S. gallons (4,500 million liters) of fuel oil; 280 million U.S. gallons (1,060 million liters) of tar, pitch, and liquid petroleum gas; 594,000 million cubic feet (16,800 million cubic meters)

TABLE 2		Million tons	% of world
Major producers of steel, 1970	European Economic Community (EEC)* of which:	138	23
	West Germany	45	8
	Britain	28	5
	France	24	4
	U.S.A.	119	20
	U.S.S.R.	116	20
	Japan	93	16
	Total	466	79
	World	594	100

Source: U.S. Bureau of Mines (10, p. 610); United Nations (44, p. 306).

* Enlarged, as of 1973: Belgium-Luxembourg, Denmark, France, Federal Republic of Germany, Irish Republic, Italy, Netherlands, United Kingdom.

of natural gas; and nearly 50,000 million kilowatt-hours of electric power. Finally, water is an important ingredient: about 10,000 million U.S. gallons (40,000 million liters) are used in the industry each day, some 5 percent of which is lost. In 1970 the United States produced about 20 percent of the world's steel. Therefore, although the raw material mix in other countries is somewhat different, one can get a rough approximation of the materials used by the world steel industry by multiplying the U.S. figures by five.

THE LOCATION OF THE STEEL INDUSTRY • Steel in one form or another is an indispensable ingredient for most of the world's industry, and steel manufactured by the processes we have outlined makes itself felt as a primary force throughout the whole structure of the economy. What is the relationship between the location of steelmaking and the geography of its raw materials?

The main raw materials, iron ore and coal, controlled the original location of the steel industry to a large extent. Most steel producing capacity was located close to these basic raw materials. In turn, centers of heavy industry were located close to steel producing capacity.

With time, however, the changing technology of steelmaking reduced the volume of raw material inputs, the transport costs on raw materials fell, and a gradual reappraisal of the best locations for the industry was made. In particular, it was recognized, especially by the industry in the United States, that the most advantageous locations were generally to be found near to the largest markets for steel, at sites where raw material assembly could be highly efficient. These locations offered not only a low-cost and efficient movement of products to customers, but they also provided a ready supply of scrap metal, which was of growing importance in the economics of the industry. Thus, with the passage of time, the dominance of Pittsburgh producers in the American industry was reduced in favor of steelmaking in the Midwest, along the East Coast, and to a lesser extent in California and Texas.

Experience in the United States has been echoed elsewhere. Of Canada, Buck and Elver (8, p. i) have written: "The most important consideration in determining the location of successful Canadian steel plants has been the size, nature and location of the present and future market for primary steel shapes and for secondary products made principally of steel." The most striking example of all is to be found in Japan, the third largest steel producer in the world. With virtually no domestic iron- and steel-making raw materials, the industry there relies upon one of the most sophisticated and economic bulk material assembly operations ever created. The Japanese producers, although they have penetrated steel markets all over the world, are located essentially to serve their country's major domestic industrial complexes; and they have chosen sites—many of them reclaimed from the sea—in or near those complexes, yet capable of exploiting the economies of bulk material transport in large ocean-going vessels.

The older iron and steel industries of Western Europe, meanwhile, have had to adjust to these new locational forces. It has not been easy. Steelworks have been built on or near the North Sea and Mediterranean coasts in order to combine good market access with efficient raw material assembly. But old traditions die hard, and there have been many difficulties in making the geographical transformation. In the older locations, where so many of the workers depend upon the steel industry for their livelihood, alternative employments are very limited. The collapse of the industry implies the virtual collapse of the community, and as a consequence social and political pressures mount to delay and minimize change. In the conflict between social and economic objectives, it is inevitable that political considerations assume a growing importance in the locational behavior of the industry.

Meanwhile, in the fully planned economies of Eastern Europe, the iron and steel industry has passed through a similar cycle of events. The first Five Year Plans of the U.S.S.R. placed considerable importance upon the development of the Soviet industry adjacent to its raw material sources in the Ukraine, the Urals, and Western Siberia, but the last decade has seen an increasing proportion of new capacity located nearer to the large markets of European Russia, at places such as Cherepovetz and Novo-Lipetsk, near Leningrad and Moscow. The growing capacity of the plants of Middle Europe—in Poland, East Germany, Czechoslovakia, and Hungary, for example—also reflects a response to local market needs and opportunities. Drawing upon

Soviet and other supplies of iron ore, and sometimes foreign coking coal, the iron and steel industries of these countries are as market-oriented as the industries in Australia, Brazil, and Sweden.

A recent RFF study concluded its analysis of the location of the iron and steel industry in these terms:

Any interpretation of the changing world geography of the iron and steel industry in the second half of the twentieth century must above all point to the strength of the locational pulls toward its markets. Under all economic systems at the international level, the market orientation of the industry was taken for granted, but it was increasingly recognized at the national level too. Technological, historical, transport, political, and sociological factors were by no means irrelevant, of course, to the geographical behavior of the industry. But . . . the all-important attraction of the industry's markets is repeatedly underlined. Only on this foundation can an understanding of the geography of iron ore demands be built. (27, p. 105)

RAW MATERIAL TRANSPORT • A key factor in this shift towards a market-oriented iron and steel industry has been the improving efficiency of raw material transport operations, which have permitted the shipment of mineral raw materials and fuels over increasing distances. During the last two decades, a combination of circumstances has greatly improved the efficiency and lowered the cost of ocean bulk transport, and so has helped to reduce greatly the importance of distance. Improvements in the methods of constructing ships, pioneered by the Japanese, have lowered the real costs of new vessels substantially. There has also been the growing use of ever-larger vessels. The 10,000-dwt. tramp ship of the early 1950s has given way to 150,000-dwt. and even 200,000-dwt. carriers; these have much reduced the costs per ton-kilometer and are particularly advantageous for long hauls.

The modern bulk carrier can also be designed to serve several trades, to carry bauxite and oil as well as iron ore. In consequence, the vessel can be used on its return haul more frequently, and complex triangular and quadrangular patterns of commodity movement can be developed—ore from Western Australia to Rotterdam, ballast to the Persian Gulf, oil to Japan, and ballast back to Australia. The previous instability of freight rates in response to vessel availability and demand has also been significantly reduced either through ownership of vessels by the iron and steel industry or through long-term charters, sometimes for fifteen and twenty years.

The full impact of these changes can be seen in one specific example. The charge for moving ore between Brazil and Japan in the middle 1950s ranged between $16 and $20 per ton; such a rate might have been negotiated on the open tramp market in times of relative shipping scarcity, and would have applied to vessels of 10,000 dwt.

Plate 1. Port Talbot, South Wales. The new tidal harbor adjacent to the integrated iron and steel works and strip mill of the British Steel Corporation is capable of handling vessels of over 125,000 dwt. Ore now travels to the 3-million-ton works and other plants in South Wales from as far away as Australia. To the left of the jetty can be seen the ore stockyards and the blast furnaces; to the right are the steel works and strip mill. (Courtesy British Steel Corporation.)

or 15,000 dwt. By the early 1960s, such charter rates for vessels of up to 20,000 dwt. in a weaker shipping market had fallen to $7 or $8 per ton. Following the opening of the new port of Tubarao, ore carriers of 70,000 dwt. could be used, and the rate fell to $5.50; subsequently, with the introduction of oil/ore carriers on a quadrangular trade in the late 1960s, the rate fell yet further to $4 per ton. Such a fall from $20 to $4 might represent an extreme case; yet declines of 50 and 60 percent in iron ore freight rates on particular runs are not difficult to find in the period 1950 to 1970.

Similar, although less dramatic, changes have also occurred in inland transport. Progress in reducing costs on the Great Lakes was limited as a consequence of somewhat stagnant market conditions there (27, p. 201). On inland waterways, however, the introduction of larger barges and the new multiple push-barge techniques afforded scale economies and falling transport rates on such famous hauls as Rotterdam to the Ruhr, and Baton Rouge to St. Louis. Progress in rail-road haulage has been much more variable. Many of the more inno-vative managements in North America and Western Europe embraced the opportunities of new railroad technology. Through increasing the size of their freight cars (wagons) to 100 tons and their trains to 50 or even 100 cars, they were able to quote remarkably competitive rates, especially when unit train principles, involving the constant use of permanently coupled cars between two fixed places, were em-ployed. The "traditional" rate for hauling ore from Mesabi to Pitts-burgh, a distance of 1,000 miles, was about $8 per ton; by the late 1960s, using unit trains and large cars, the rate for the somewhat shorter haul of 700 miles between Mesabi and Granite City (St. Louis) was as little as $4 per ton.

Pipelines have also been used for the first time in recent years to transport iron ore—for example, in Tasmania (Southern Australia) be-tween the mine at Savage River and the pellet plant and ocean termi-nal at Brickmakers Bay—and they clearly have a role to play in the industry's operations. Where the terrain is mountainous and the ore not too abrasive, pipelines carrying iron ore in a slurry can frequently be associated with a terminal beneficiation plant. The experimental, and apparently successful, ocean transport of ore slurry, which has been pioneered between Peru and Japan, possibly suggests a widening market for ore pipelines in the future.

The quality, speed, capacity, and cost of the transport links be-tween the iron and steel industry and the mines that serve it have assumed a new role in the economic geography of iron ore production. As a consequence of recent progress, and especially following the extraordinary changes in ocean freight rates, iron ore deposits and mines that are situated fairly close to deepwater port facilities have been given a new competitive advantage over many of the ore bodies that were traditionally used to serve the iron and steel industry. It is not the only factor that has led to a reassessment of the worth of some ore bodies—the basic oxygen converter, for example, has placed a premium upon low-phosphorous ores—but it is certainly one of the most influential. Between 1950 and 1971, the amount of seaborne ore traffic rose nearly twentyfold from 120,000 to some 2,220,000 million ton-kilometers (figure 3).

IRON ORE (in which the supply of available raw materials has broadened greatly in answer to a threatened shortage) • The pattern of iron ore supply has been transformed in recent years not only by the reassessment of distance occasioned by declining bulk transport costs and the changing geography of the iron and steel industry both within and between countries, but also by the steadily growing size of both activities (figure 4). World production of steel increased from 192 million tons in 1950 to 593 million tons in 1970. Individual steel plants increased in size—at the top end of an admittedly wide scale—from 1–2 million ingot tons capacity to 10–16 million tons capacity. Ocean ore carriers and ore trains became larger, as has been seen. Iron ore mines increased in size—again, at the top end of the scale—from 1–2 million tons to 10 million tons and over. The Reserve Mining Company at Silver Bay, Minnesota, for example, extracts over 25 million tons of rock each year to produce its 9 million tons of pellets; and the UGOK mine in the Krivoy Rog mining district of the U.S.S.R. handles over 25 million tons of crude magnetite to produce 11.4 million tons of concentrate. World production of iron ore increased from 116 million tons of contained iron in 1950 to 419 million tons in 1970; actual tonnage output grew from 244 to 767 million tons.

In the years immediately following World War II, especially in the United States and the countries of Western Europe, concern was widespread about the future adequacy of ore supplies for the iron and steel industry. With iron the second most abundant metal in the earth's crust, in retrospect this was somewhat surprising. The fears stemmed from the accelerating use of existing reserves, and they generated a threefold response: the search for new ore bodies, the upgrading of low-grade ores, and the development of new transport technologies to allow the iron and steel industry to reach out to more distant sources of ore at no great increase in its raw material costs, which has already been discussed.

New Ore Bodies. Perhaps the most important response to the fear of ore shortage was the search for new ore bodies. The iron and steel industries of North America and Western Europe sent their geologists into the unexplored parts of their own continents, into Africa, into Latin America, and into Asia; and they reaped a lush harvest. New ore

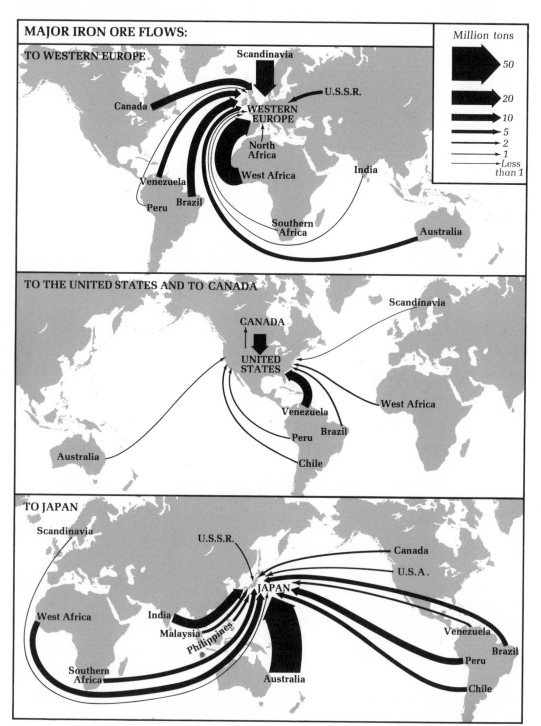

Figure 3. World seaborne trade in iron ore, 1971. The flow of Australian ore to Japan is a relatively recent development. North American figures include trade on the Great Lakes. *Source:* Fearnley and Egers Chartering Company, Oslo.

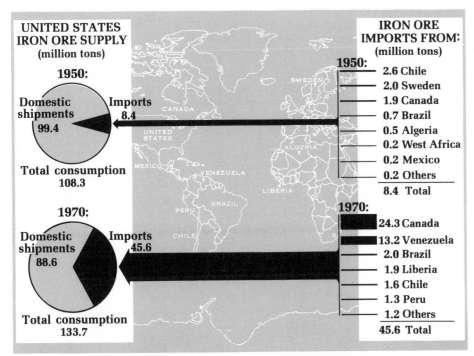

UNITED STATES
IRON ORE SUPPLY
(million tons)

1950:

Domestic shipments 99.4

Imports 8.4

Total consumption 108.3

1970:

Domestic shipments 88.6

Imports 45.6

Total consumption 133.7

IRON ORE
IMPORTS FROM:
(million tons)

1950:
2.6 Chile
2.0 Sweden
1.9 Canada
0.7 Brazil
0.5 Algeria
0.2 West Africa
0.2 Mexico
0.2 Others
8.4 Total

1970:
24.3 Canada
13.2 Venezuela
2.0 Brazil
1.9 Liberia
1.6 Chile
1.3 Peru
1.2 Others
45.6 Total

Figure 4. Production of steel in the major regions of the world, 1950, 1960, and 1970. In twenty years each of the major regions of the world has greatly increased its production of steel. But the rates of growth have varied and the performance of Japan has been outstanding. *Source:* United Nations, appropriate years (44) and Manners (27).

deposits were found in such countries as Venezuela, Canada, Guinea, Mauretania, and Peru, deposits which previously had not entered into the industry's estimates of its reserves. At the same time, the U.S.S.R. embarked upon a search for further ore supplies in its vast territory and proved the existence of enormous reserves. China and India also explored for, and found, new sources of ore. Indeed, the developing world as a whole, anxious to exploit its natural resources in a search for economic growth, was only too eager to take up the search for ore. With government financial assistance, considerable reserves of ore were found in Liberia, in Swaziland, and in Brazil, among other developing countries.

As new ore deposits continued to be found in rapid succession, from the Yukon Territory to Uruguay, and from the Ukraine to Angola, the world iron and steel industry saw its reserves of ore mount steadily. In 1950, the United Nations had estimated world reserves to be 26,719 million tons of contained iron; by 1966, when the United Nations published another survey, the figure had been revised upwards to 114,400 million tons of contained iron (table 3). From a situation of potential

TABLE 3	Region and country	Reserves	Potential reserves
World iron ore reserves, 1966 estimates (*million tons, Fe content*)	World	114,400	83,000
	North America	16,900	28,400
	Canada	4,200	6,500
	U.S.A.	12,700	21,900
	Western Europe	7,100	2,200
	E.E.C.	3,200	400
	France	2,700	
	Luxembourg	100	
	West Germany	400	400
	Austria	100	
	Britain	800	
	Norway	300	400
	Portugal	100	
	Spain	600	600
	Sweden	1,800	
	Yugoslavia	200	400
	Eastern Europe	44,800	4,300
	Middle Europe	200	
	Bulgaria	100	
	Poland	100	
	U.S.S.R.	44,600	4,300
	Latin America	30,600	22,900
	Argentina	100	
	Bolivia		11,100
	Brazil	28,200	9,600
	Chile	400	1,000
	Cuba		1,200
	Mexico	300	
	Peru	200	
	Venezuela	1,300	large
	Central America		large

scarcity in the late 1940s, therefore, the iron ore reserves position of the iron and steel industry had been transformed within fifteen years to what could only be regarded as an astoundingly bountiful resource base. The United Nations figure of 1966 is equivalent to nearly 300 years' supply, at the 1970 level of consumption. The remarkable thing about this achievement is that the new reserves of iron ore are clearly available to the iron and steel industry at no significant increase in costs—indeed, in recent years the market for iron ore has been characterized by falling prices.

New Enrichment Techniques. The development of new beneficiating and agglomeration technologies, which would allow the use of grades of ore previously regarded as unsuitable for the blast furnace, has been

Region and country	Reserves	Potential reserves
Asia	4,300	16,200
Communist Asia		1,300
China		1,300
Non-Communist Asia	4,300	14,900
India	4,200	12,600
Laos		600
Pakistan	100	
Others		large*
Oceania	4,700	3,600
Australia	4,400	3,300
New Caledonia		large
New Zealand	300	300
Africa and Middle East	6,000	5,400
Algeria	100	600
Angola	100	
Congo		3,200
Egypt	100	100
Gabon	600	large
Guinea	100	500
Liberia	300	200
Libya	200	600
Mauretania	100	100
Morocco		100
Nigeria	100	
Rhodesia		large
South Africa	4,300	large
Others		large*

Source: Manners (27, pp. 240–241).
Note: Reserves exclude China; potential reserves include 1945 estimates for China.
* Especially Java and New Guinea in Asia; Cameroons and Central African Republic in Africa.

particularly successful in the U.S.S.R., Canada, and the United States. At the Soviet Union's Olenyogorsk mine, for example, an ore body with an average ore content of 32 percent iron, the rock is treated in such a way as to produce concentrates of 69 and 64 percent iron. In another set of ore preparation processes, known as agglomeration technology, the two principal techniques that have been developed are sintering and pelletizing. In both cases, not only is ore upgraded in terms of its iron content, but its physical structure is improved in such a way as to ensure a better performance in the blast furnace. Once commercial production had begun, it was quickly recognized that, though the iron-rich pellets might (in dollars per ton) be more costly than traditional ore, they also permitted savings in other phases of the pig-iron–making process. They were higher in grade, cheaper to handle and ship, did not freeze during shipping, required less fuel to smelt, and were altogether a superior blast furnace charge. The use of these prepared charges, some of which even include lime so that they are self-fluxing, can as much as double the capacity of a blast furnace, and their production has increased greatly. Simultaneously, the resource base of the iron and steel industry has been dramatically widened as a result of these outstanding technological achievements.

Today's Pattern of Iron Ore Production. The new pattern of demand, plus the new possibilities of supply, helped to transform the pattern of iron ore production during the last two decades. In 1950, out of a world production of 116 million tons of contained iron in iron ore, the U.S. mining industry, with 49 million tons, dominated world production; and over 80 percent of its output came from the mines of the Lake Superior region. The other large producers in 1950 were the U.S.S.R. (23 million tons), where the industry was highly localized in the Ukraine and the Urals, France (10 million tons), and Sweden (8 million tons); Britain, with an output of nearly 4 million tons, produced almost as much iron ore as either Latin America or Asia or Africa. By 1970, world output had increased to 419 million contained tons. The largest producer by far was the U.S.S.R., with 106 million tons (table 4). The output of the United States on the other hand had increased only slightly to 53 million tons, while that of Canada had increased dramatically from 2 million to 30 million tons. In Western Europe, France (18 million tons) and Sweden (20 million tons) retained their importance, but elsewhere in the world a series of new producers had arrived on the scene. In Latin America, Brazil (20 million tons) and Venezuela (14 million tons) were the most important; in Asia, the leaders were China (22 million tons) and India (20 million tons); and two other leading producers were Australia (33 million tons) and Liberia (15 million tons). This new geography reflects how quickly mineral supply patterns can change.

TABLE 4		Million tons	% of world
Major producers of	U.S.S.R.	106	25
iron ore, 1970	U.S.A.	53	13
(iron-in-ore)	Australia	33	8
	Canada	30	7
	China	22	5
	Brazil	20	5
	Sweden	20	5
	India	20	5
	Total	304	73
	World	419	100

Source: United Nations (44, p. 167).

Plate 2. Mount Tom Price, Western Australia. The crushing and screening plant associated with the iron ore mining complex at Mount Tom Price. Working in conjunction with a train loading station, this plant serves four open pits and the entire complex produces some 22.5 million tons of iron ore pellets annually. The complex is linked to the port of Dampier by a 182-mile railroad. (Courtesy RTZ [Rio Tinto Zinc].)

QUESTIONS OF SELF-SUFFICIENCY • Although global resources of iron ore are now clearly more than adequate, the resource situation for individual countries is more uncertain and poses important problems. The U.S.S.R. aimed for, and clearly has achieved, resource self-sufficiency in iron ore. The United States, on the other hand, has moved from a situation in which it was once comfortably self-sufficient, boasting some of the wealthiest reserves of ore in the world, to a position in which the country now imports one-third of its requirements (figure 5). This raises the issue of national mineral self-sufficiency.

To many people, a self-sufficient country is one which supplies from within its borders all its requirements of a particular substance. In the same way, a farmer of some generations ago, who produced all his own food and clothing, was considered self-sufficient. In this sense, the United States used to be self-sufficient in iron ore, in copper, in oil, and in a number of other mineral commodities. But since the nation now imports significant quantities of each of these materials, its situation has changed. Some may feel that self-sufficiency in basic commodities is a highly desirable condition and that the United States should aim at providing its total domestic supply from its own resources even if it involves a higher cost than does the acquisition of some key materials on the world market. However, a broader concept of self-sufficiency can be applied to a society which is capable of producing enough of a raw material for its needs, if this were necessary, but which finds it more economic to import some of it. Not only can such a course bring economic advantages but it can also conserve domestic sources of some raw materials for future use.

The question of whether it is better to increase supplies of raw materials from marginal or submarginal domestic sources, or to import them, offers endless argument. Yet political decisions, taken deliberately or by default, cannot be evaded. Degrees of self-sufficiency can be and are decided and modified by security considerations, expressed in government programs of stockpiling, subsidies, standby facilities, tariffs and quotas, and other actions to maintain or stimulate mineral development and production. The question of the relative cost of these measures to society as a whole is among the most complex in social accounting.

Perhaps the most remarkable feature of the American iron and steel industry's growing dependence upon iron ore imports has been the absence of an accompanying public debate. Unlike the question of oil imports, which has been discussed extensively in recent years, or the debate about steel product imports, to which there was a very positive political response, the growing dependence upon foreign iron ore has never caught the imagination of the press or the politicians. Yet the policy options are there. Although the years since World War II have seen the discovery of relatively few high-grade ore

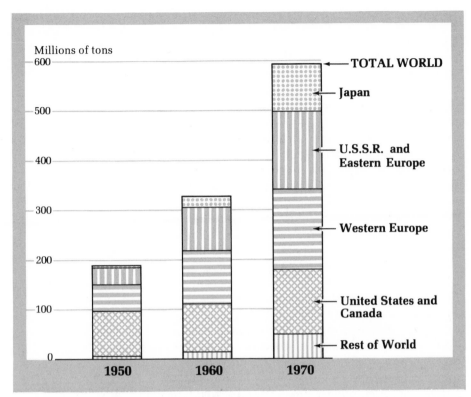

Figure 5. Sources of iron ore for the United States steel industry, 1950 and 1970. As demand for steel increases, and mineral supply economics change, the United States is drawing upon foreign sources for larger amounts of its iron ore supplies. *Source:* Bureau of Mines (10).

bodies in the United States, the economics of pellet production based upon the taconite and jasperite ore of the Lake Superior region have afforded an adequate resource base for a much higher level of self-sufficiency than at present exists. Indeed, with the adoption of advanced railroad technology and management, it might be argued that self-sufficiency could be achieved over a number of years with no significant increase in the industry's delivered raw material costs. The industry, however, has taken a different course, an explanation of which can be found in the combination of a number of factors, as follows:

• Immediately after World War II, when the fear of an impending ore shortage was widespread, and when modern beneficiating techniques were not yet available, the steel industry found *alternative sources* of acceptable ore in Canada and in Venezuela. Some degree of choice was therefore preempted, for once having opened up mines there it was difficult for the industry to find an economic case to close them down while their costs remained reasonably competitive. This was particularly true since the *vertical integration* of much iron and steel and iron ore production means that most imports are primarily corporate activities rather than commercial transactions and there are no interested parties waiting to oppose an upsurge of imports. Beyond this, the industry, and presumably the government, judged that the overseas sources of ore that had been found and opened up were (and would remain) strategically safe.

• Approaching the problem from another angle, in the past there had been a tendency for those domestic states with abundant ore resources to lean heavily on the iron ore industry for tax revenue. In response, the companies insisted upon the "Taconite Amendment" (a Minnesota constitutional guarantee that ensures taxes on the iron ore industry will not exceed the general level of company taxation in the state); also they decided that ore *supplies from a diversity of sources* would be in their better commercial interest. From the point of view of the producer, overseas ore supplies permit an integrated iron ore and iron and steel producer to *sell surplus ore on the world market* in years of depressed market conditions at home. This is an option only occasionally available to the landlocked producers of the Lake Superior region. Also, any attempt to build up domestic production to meet most domestic needs would have been achieved in the first instance only at the price of very great *capital expenditures* and, in some parts of the country, more expensive ore; this was a situation the industry did not want to afford.

• And finally, even in the 1950s the first expressions of *concern over the "environment"* were being heard and pressures were beginning to be exerted on mining companies to modify activities such as large open-pit mines which damaged the landscape.

It can be seen, therefore, how a multiplicity of corporate decisions led to a decision by the American iron and steel industry as a whole to rely increasingly upon foreign sources of iron ore. Whether, in the context of a mounting foreign trade deficit, an analysis of the needs of the whole industry would have arrived at the same conclusion is clearly an open question.

4 THE ALLOYING ELEMENTS:
which illustrate some of the ways of responding to the characteristics of fixed location

OVER 90 percent of the steel made is carbon steel, iron metal which contains a small amount of carbon (usually less than 1 percent). The presence of this carbon changes the properties of iron, thereby making it a much stronger and harder metal. A typical carbon steel might contain 0.25 percent carbon, 0.45 percent manganese, 0.1 percent silicon, and lesser amounts of phosphorus and sulfur. By changing the proportions of these different elements it is possible to change the characteristics of carbon steel.

Carbon alone, however, cannot supply all of the characteristics that make steel of value to modern industry. The other 10 percent of steel production consists of alloy steels—steels to which have been added carefully measured amounts of one or a number of alloying elements such as nickel, chromium, or vanadium, to alter their strength, toughness, or resistance to corrosion. Stainless steel is perhaps the most familiar of this group.

There are about a dozen principal alloying elements, which can be used in varying amounts and in varying combinations to obtain an almost infinite variety of steels. Quantities may range from as little as 0.0005 percent of boron in certain boron alloy steels to as much as 27 percent chromium in certain stainless steels. In most alloy steels, though, the alloying elements are present in quantities of less than 2 percent.

Although the alloying mineral in an alloy steel is relatively small, its use is so necessary that the mining of alloying elements is a vitally important industry in many parts of the world. Some idea of the role played by these alloys is indicated by the following extract:

Constructional alloy steel derives its usual strength and toughness from the addition of wonder-working alloys to steel in the form of ferro-alloys during melting, plus subsequent heat treatment of the steel to provide the full beneficial effects of these alloys. A typical composition might include these elements in the following percentages: carbon .15; manganese .75; silicon .24; nickel .85; chromium .50; molybdenum .45; copper .30; vanadium .05; and boron .003. (14, p. 3)

As alloys go, this one is relatively complicated. The carbon, silicon, copper, and boron that go into it are materials whose major uses lie outside the steel industry. The other elements, though, are typical alloying metals produced mainly for use in the steel industry. In this chapter consideration is given to these five elements: manganese, nickel, chromium, molybdenum, and vanadium.

MANGANESE (in which is indicated the response of a major consuming country with virtually no domestic reserves of an essential material) • For every ton of steel produced in the United States, an average of some 36 pounds (16 kilograms) of manganese arrive at the steel furnace or ladle in the form of ferroalloy, ore, manganese metal, pig iron, scrap, and recycled slag—yet only 12 pounds remain in each final ingot ton. Manganese enters the steelmaking process at a number of stages and in a number of forms. Some goes into the blast furnace as a minor constituent of iron ore. The greatest part of the manganese is added in the steel furnace: some as the manganese content of the scrap component, some contained in the slag left from previous heats, and some as ferromanganese, a product made by treating manganese ore in a blast furnace. Most of the manganese in the steel furnace is used to remove sulfur, and over half of it ends up in the furnace slag. Some does go through into the finished steel, though, and at the end of the refining process the manganese content of the molten steel might be expected to be 0.05 to 0.35 percent. These percentages are too low even for plain carbon steel, which normally would be expected to run about 0.5 percent manganese. So manganese in the form of ferromanganese is again added in the ladle after the furnace has been tapped. At this stage manganese can also be added to produce what are sometimes termed manganese alloy steels—the steels that contain more than 1.65 percent manganese and are stronger, harder, and better able to resist abrasion. Steel with 12 percent and more manganese content is extremely tough. Crushers, power-shovel teeth, and well-drill bits are among the uses for this material.

Manganese is an essential material with which the United States is remarkably poorly supplied. The country has no domestic reserves of commercial significance, and the one mine that did produce manganese ore, concentrate, or nodules closed down in 1970. Yet the value of the manganese consumed in the United States, after it has been converted from ore into ferroalloys, amounts to more than the worth of all the other ferroalloys combined. About one-third of the world's known reserves of manganese are located in the Soviet Union, especially in the Chiatura and Nikopol districts. The U.S.S.R., which mined some 38 percent (7.0 million tons) of the world output in 1970, is the only major industrial power that is self-sufficient in this key mineral. Elsewhere the two major producers, both with a rapidly expanding output, are South Africa and Brazil. Additional supplies come from India, Gabon, and China. These six countries among them accounted for over 84 percent of world production in 1970 (table 5). Where, then, does the United States procure its supplies?

As Brooks (3, p. 24) has pointed out in an RFF study, "The pattern of world trade in manganese is strongly influenced by two factors: direct foreign investment and political constraints." For many years the steel companies of the United States (like those of Western Europe) did not invest directly in manganese ore production. Before World War II supplies were always abundant. Apart from the large U.S.S.R. deposits, most mines were at that time within the British Commonwealth and Empire—India, the Gold Coast (now Ghana), and South Africa—and they were under the control of British mining firms. After World War II, however, that political sphere began to disintegrate. In 1948 the U.S.S.R. cut off manganese supplies to the United States. Ore prices became unstable. And, in response, the American steel industry decided to develop its own manganese deposits (through either partial or total ownership) in Gabon and Brazil. Today its imports come especially, but not exclusively, from captive sources there. Although it is said that the U.S.S.R. would now be willing to sell manganese ore to the United States, the latter for obvious reasons has declined

TABLE 5		*Thousand tons*	*% of world*
Major producers of	U.S.S.R.	6,985	38
manganese ore, 1970	South Africa	2,680	14
	Brazil	1,929	10
	India	1,651	9
	Gabon	1,453	8
	China	998	5
	Total	15,696	84
	World	18,498	100

Source: U.S. Bureau of Mines (10, p. 698).

to reopen this trade. These shifts in the pattern of trade, however, have served the United States well, if the price of manganese is any guide. Prices today are at nearly the same level as they were during the 1940s and, in terms of its relationship to the general price level, manganese is cheaper today than it was thirty years ago.

Besides this reliance upon overseas sources of manganese, the American iron and steel industry has reacted to the poverty of its domestic resources in several other ways. First, the industry has tended to design its plants and production processes in such a way as to use no more manganese than is necessary to achieve the desired standards, although there is evidence that this can be cut down still further. By contrast, it is reported that the Russians, with an abundance of manganese, consume up to four times as much manganese per ton of steel as do Americans. Some of this manganese presumably is used to substitute for elements, like molybdenum, which are relatively scarce in Russia; some may be used as a desulfurizer, permitting less strict control in the furnace; and some very likely goes to strengthen and improve the quality of their regular carbon steel.

The U.S. steel industry uses manganese rather carefully, partly because of its cost and partly because of fear of the interruption of supply. The government, which can be expected to be more concerned with strategic considerations than is industry, has taken additional steps to assure long-range supply. Stockpiling is one such step; large quantities of manganese ore and ferromanganese are kept available in case foreign sources are cut off. In 1970 the stockpile was equivalent to just under five years' supply (chapter 5, table 14).

The United States government also supports the search for and investigation of low-grade domestic resources which cannot be used economically at today's market values for manganese but could be useful were other sources to be cut off. It does this by offering premium prices and by encouraging research to develop techniques by which beneficiating costs can be reduced to a level where such materials will be more competitive. In addition, the government, in cooperation with industry, has carried out research aimed at recovering the very large amounts of manganese that are in the slag dumps of the steel mills. These dumps may run to almost 10 percent manganese and, should it ever become economic to recover this material, they would be a large source of the mineral. Development of this potential resource has been slowed in recent years, however, by the growing use of the basic oxygen converter rather than the open-hearth process in steelmaking; slag from the latter has a much higher manganese content. Moreover, even the most attractive of the several processes using low-grade ores and slag seems to be incapable of yielding manganese at a cost less than three times the present imported value—and would add 1 percent to the cost of a ton of steel. Both these impediments suggest that the above alternative resources might better be termed latent than marginal.

In addition to these responses to sparse domestic resources, an unusual new source of manganese is also being actively considered for development. Analysis has shown that nodules on the ocean floor contain manganese as well as other minerals. Nodules off the southeast coast of the United States at depths of 500 to 3,000 feet (15 to 900 meters) average about 20 percent manganese, and others may go up to 50 percent. Some authorities (3, p. 110) believe that this source is not only the largest but also the least expensive of the currently non-commercial sources of manganese. However, until deep sea mining is actually attempted, the question of its competitive standing must remain unresolved. The nodules also contain iron, nickel, cobalt, and copper. If such materials can be mined and processed economically—a good deal of speculation on equipment and operating procedures has gone on—and if international cooperation can be achieved as to their equitable development, it will completely change the supply pattern of the world, not only for manganese, but perhaps for a number of other metals.

The success of the American iron and steel industry's response to its poor manganese resource base at home can be seen by reference to the metal's ready availability in adequate quantities over the last twenty years or so, and its increased price stability. The fact that none of the strictly domestic sources has proved economic, despite considerable effort and public money, is not a total loss: the technology developed clearly has a political value, for it demonstrates that within a few years the United States, at a price, could become self-sufficient in manganese if it so desired. To cover that intermediate period, the stockpile obviously plays a key role. This is the best means of covering short-term crises in manganese supply, and its size can be altered with the unfolding of international political events. In the meantime, American reliance upon foreign sources can be seen to have a valuable role to play in world affairs. Many of the newer producers of manganese ore are relatively underdeveloped and rely upon their mineral exports for earning foreign exchange, a crucial element in their plans for growth. Had the United States elected to pay the price of manganese self-sufficiency, or were it to do so in the future, this in turn would detrimentally affect the progress of several developing economies. As Brooks has put it:

The problem of the twentieth century is, after peace, the problem of underdevelopment. Here (in the case of manganese) it arises in stark form because technologic progress in the form of a potential to utilize low-grade and nonconventional mineral resources conflicts with development. There is no easy answer to this problem. Further study should be devoted to the introduction of such technologic advances *and techniques that might be devised to cushion the shock. Under-development is a cost that, in one way or another, must be taken into account. (3, p. 115)*

This theme of the interrelationships between governments and the mineral industry is taken up again, in some detail, in chapter 5.

NICKEL (in which responses to fluctuations in mineral demand are noted and the scale of a modern mining community is indicated) • Nickel, another important alloying element, is widely used in stainless steel, in heat-resisting steel for such things as high-pressure pipes and steam lines, in alloy steels for automotive and machinery parts, and in a series of nonferrous alloys such as Monel metal (67 percent nickel, 30 percent copper). Nickel in steel increases toughness, strength, and ductility, and can add a great deal to the attractive appearance of the steel product.

The history of man's use of nickel has been a series of ups and downs which has continued to the present. The medieval miners in Saxony, who gave nickel its name, thought they were dealing with a copper ore; and when their smelters yielded a hard, white metal, which was difficult to work, they called it *Kupfernickel*—the devil's copper. Nickel was later isolated, but it received little attention, and world production was small until late in the last century. In 1883 construction workers, carving a path for the roadbed of the Canadian Pacific Railway through the barren rocks of Northern Ontario, encountered an outcrop of what they considered to be a copper ore. They had discovered the deposits of the Sudbury Basin. It soon became apparent that these copper deposits were also rich in nickel and that the nickel had to be separated before either metal could be marketed. This left the producers with large amounts of nickel for which there was no ready market. However, since nickel appeared to have useful properties, a search began to find uses for this metal. By 1902, two of the major companies in the area, the Orford Copper Company and the Canadian Copper Company, amalgamated; recognizing that they were no longer really copper companies, they changed their name to the International Nickel Company of Canada, Limited (INCO).

Since discovery of the Sudbury Basin deposits, Canada has been the major nickel-producing country in the world (currently about 41 percent of total production), and International Nickel has been the largest nickel-producing company (table 6). It has twelve mines, five concentrators, and two smelters in the Sudbury area, and other facilities both in Canada and overseas. The other major producers in the world are the U.S.S.R. and the French island of New Caledonia in the Pacific. Extensive nickel reserves exist in Australia and Indonesia (both with the prospect of becoming significant producers), and also in the Philippines, the Dominican Republic, and in Cuba where, until the

TABLE 6		Thousand tons	% of world
Major producers	Canada	277	45
of nickel, 1970	U.S.S.R.	110	18
	New Caledonia	105	17
	Australia	28	5
	Indonesia	18	3
	Total	538	88
	World	621	100

Source: U.S. Bureau of Mines (10, p. 790).

revolution, the United States government was active in their development.

The first major market for nickel to be developed by researchers was in the manufacture of armaments, for it was discovered that nickel alloy steels made superior armor plate. Military needs have remained important to nickel producers and can, in fact, be used in analyzing the cycles through which the demand for nickel has passed; for the relation between nickel supply and demand has been an irregular one, with fluctuations that are extreme even for the volatile mineral industries.

The demand for nickel for armor plating grew rapidly as the world moved into World War I, only to collapse when the war ended (Canadian production in 1918 was over 42,000 tons, but had dropped to about 8,000 tons by 1922). Active research, largely carried out by INCO, led to the development of many peacetime markets, so that by 1929 the demand was over 50,000 tons. Output continued to increase into World War II when a new Canadian peak of 131,000 tons was reached in 1943, but this was followed by a period of surplus capacity during the postwar years. Another surge of demand came with the Korean War, and new capacity was developed under the stimulus of government support. Again this was followed by a period of surplus capacity, which lasted until a combination of the stockpiling program of the United States government and escalation of the war in Vietnam caused a further upward surge of demand. The tight supply position in the non-Communist world during the middle and late 1960s was further aggravated by unusually long strikes in the Canadian industry in 1969. However, by the early 1970s new mining and smelting capacity had been constructed and the market was reasonably well balanced once again. The prolonged period of shortages in the late 1960s had meanwhile encouraged not only a rise in nickel prices but also much vigorous exploration and resource development in many parts of the world—in the Caribbean, in Africa, in Australia, and in the U.S.S.R., as well as in Canada. And all the evidence was pointing to the probability of a surplus of nickel capacity once again within a few years.

Some of the reasons for this somewhat repetitive pattern are unique to the nickel industry. The unusual surges of demand placed on nickel producers by military users (and more recently by the United States' stockpiling program), and the subsequent supply stringency while new capacity was being developed, are not associated with all metals. Likewise, the amount of idle capacity that in the past has characterized nickel mining and smelting after a slackening of military demands is also unusual. On the other hand, all the mineral and metal industries are subject to fluctuations in the rate at which their markets expand; and even a periodic fall in demand, in phase with the trade cycle, is not an unusual experience.

At the same time, the provision of new capacity—that is, the opening up of new mines and the construction of new smelters—has two important characteristics. First, it needs a considerable lead-time. The process of looking for, finding, appraising, developing, and bringing a new mine into production can take from six to ten years, and even longer. Second, mining investment is "lumpy" and new production capacity has to be made available in large blocks. While a moderate degree of excess production capacity reassures the consumer, a large mine and smelter that are newly brought into operation can tip capacity steeply upwards and create a substantial surplus. In turn, this can generate serious economic problems for the industry, such as a low rate of return on capital, a softening of product prices, and the need to lay off some labor.

These two features, fluctuating demand and lumpiness of investment, mean that the mining and metal industries have some difficulty in keeping production capacity reasonably in line with demand for any length of time. Constant changes in the relationship between the two is a normal feature of both industries. Nickel, because its producers are small in number and its uses are largely military, illustrates the pattern more clearly than most other metals.

Thus the somewhat paradoxical situation of nickel producers expanding their production capacity at a time when existing capacity is being only partially used is not without economic logic. For example, in 1958, with excess capacity stimulated by the stockpiling program, INCO had facilities in the Sudbury Basin to produce about 140,000 tons of nickel, but was called upon to supply only a little over 90,000 tons, an obvious case of overcapacity. Yet in 1958 the company was well on the way to developing a new nickel producing area in northern Manitoba—second in size in the world only to INCO's Sudbury operations—which was to add another 34,000 tons of nickel to the world's producing capacity in 1961.

The development of this new Thompson property in Manitoba was begun in 1956. At the time, existing capacity was well in excess of demand, but market forecasts suggested that new capacity would be needed by 1961. As evidence of the validity of these forecasts,

Plate 3. Thompson, Manitoba, Canada. In the foreground is the town of Thompson, built to serve the mining and smelting complex of the International Nickel Company of Canada, Ltd., seen in the background. (Courtesy INCO.)

INCO delivered a record 169,000 tons of nickel in 1961, when growing capacity, including the Thompson mine, had reached 174,000 tons. Not all of the nickel delivered was newly mined material, so demand of this order did not crowd the newly expanded capacity. However, it was sufficient to encourage further investment in the area and by 1972 a second mine had been completed and two additional mines were also under construction; these would bring the capacity of INCO's Manitoba operations to 77,000 tons of nickel each year. Meanwhile the company had already built a smelter and a refinery at Thompson, to make it the first such integrated facility in the world. In fact, with increasing populations, rising levels of living, and the demand for new materials arising from advancing technology in such areas as transportation, electronics, and chemicals, the demand for nickel has increased steadily in all the developed economies. The producers of the metal have been quite hard pressed to keep sufficiently ahead of demand and thus retain the confidence of users.

The Thompson project is especially interesting for it includes one of the newest of the world's "mining towns," those isolated communities which provide homes and services for miners. Often in the past they have become "ghost towns" when minable material runs out, but the town of Thompson has an air of permanence. It is located some 400 miles (640 kilometers) north of Winnipeg, in an area of rock, forest, and lakes some 30 miles from the nearest railroad. Initially, all material and equipment had to be moved in by tractor trains across the frozen lakes and rivers. But a large mining operation must have employees, and the families of these employees must be able to live with them in an acceptable environment. It is to the advantage of both men and company that this be so. By 1957 a rail spur had been built to connect the mine with the railhead, and in 1958 the first homes were built on the banks of a pleasant river, about 1½ miles from the mining operations.

Today a carefully planned community, with modern homes, shopping and recreational facilities, and schools, has been erected in this wilderness—a far cry from frontier mining towns, but still an unusual place to live. By the end of 1961, some 3,500 people were living in Thompson; by 1971, the population was about 19,000. The town is not company owned. However, the nickel company has had to subsidize the community heavily, particularly in the early years, and by 1970 it had spent some $15 million on the development of the townsite. By that date the total Thompson development cost was over $550 million, of which more than 75 percent had been financed by the company; most of the additional expenditure represents public funds invested in an associated power station at Kelsey some 58 miles (90 kilometers) away, and the original rail spur, which has been extended 48 miles to the new mines. Water, sewers, electricity, schools, a hospital, a fire station—all these and more were provided, either by the company or with the company's financial assistance, to get the community off to a good start. These additional costs, which must ultimately be assessed against mineral production, are not unusual in the mining industry. The need to construct new communities in isolated areas greatly increases the costs of mineral development, the complications, and the responsibilities; but, as with Mohammed, if the mineral bearing mountain will not come to man, man must go to the mountain, wherever it chances to be.

Projects like that at Thompson—and if anything they are tending to get larger, such are the scale economies of mining, metal refining, and community service provision these days—endow the mineral industry with one of its more distinctive characteristics. Because mineral production capacity increases in a series of major steps, it tends to fluctuate widely around (rather than closely in phase with) changes in demand. Where the market is very large, as in the case of iron ore, the effect is less noticeable; the capacity of a single new mine can be more rapidly absorbed and the associated costs of underutilization (industry-wide) are easier to bear. Where the total market is relatively small, however, as in the case of nickel, the effects and the costs are more dramatically exposed.

CHROMIUM (in which captive mines are an important element in the pattern of supply, and in which the flow of ore has been uniquely altered by an international political decision) • Although chromium may be thought of mainly as a plating material used on bathroom fixtures, automobile accessories, etc., it is much more widely used as an alloying element. Small amounts of chromium add strength and hardness to steel even at high temperatures, and larger amounts turn easy-to-rust iron into corrosion-resistant stainless steel (typically 18 percent chromium, 8 percent nickel). There are other uses. In the United States, about one-fifth of the consumption of chromite, the only commercial chromium mineral, goes into the manufacture of refractories—chemically neutral bricks that are used in furnace linings, often in steel plants. In addition, about 15 percent of the chromite is used by the chemical industry in the manufacture of paint, in leather tanning, in electroplating, and the like.

This is another alloying material in which some of the world's largest steel producers—the United States, Japan, West Germany, Britain, and France, for example—are deficient. Some low-grade deposits of chromite exist in Montana, but U.S. domestic production never accounted for more than 10 percent of normal consumption and it ceased entirely in 1961. Most of the world reserves are in the eastern hemisphere, large deposits being known in the U.S.S.R., the Republic of South Africa, the Philippines, Turkey, and Rhodesia. Their long-term

TABLE 7			*Thousand tons*	*% of world*
Major producers of	U.S.S.R.		1,750	30
chromite, 1970	South Africa		1,427	24
	Philippines		576	10
	Turkey		477	8
	Albania		454	8
	Rhodesia		363	6
		Total	5,067	85
	World		5,920	100

Source: U.S. Bureau of Mines (10, p. 302).

adequacy is unchallenged. These same countries, plus Albania, are also current leaders in world production (table 7).

Chromite traditionally came from many sources and from many mines, some of which were quite small. Because of the nature of their operations, supply from individual small mines can be unreliable. In Turkey, for example, where hundreds of small mines contribute to production, the amount of material available in any one year cannot be accurately predicted. So, in order to assure themselves of a steady, predictable supply of raw material, steel companies using chromite and the large ferroalloy companies supplying chromite to industry have been developing their own properties. These are captive mines, and this backward integration towards raw materials is a trend through-out most of the mineral industry. While it solves some problems, especially in affording a greater degree of price stability, it tends also to create a number of others.

The United States is the largest importer of chromite; its large ferroalloy companies handling chromite, such as Union Carbide and the Foote Mineral Company, control many such captive mines. Union Carbide, for example, has six foreign affiliates concerned with mining chromite in Rhodesia and the Republic of South Africa. These mines, wholly or partially owned by the marketing company, can be expected to supply the bulk of the material needed by their parent companies, leaving a much smaller part of the market to be supplied by inde-pendent producers. Companies establish captive mines where there are good deposits and where the politico-economic environment seems favorable. As a result, countries that do not encourage the estab-lishment of mines controlled by foreign companies, such as Turkey, have been hard put to find a market for some of their mineral produc-tion. Turkish chromite exports to the United States dropped from nearly 500,000 tons in 1956 to about 136,000 tons in 1961; subsequently, this trade increased again to 233,000 tons in 1970—a period of chromium scarcity. Meantime, however, imports from the Republic of South Africa, where there is captive production, had increased to 369,000 tons. We do not suggest that this shift is entirely due to captive mine production—the African mines may be richer and may produce at lower cost than those of Turkey—but it is nevertheless a factor, and an increasingly important factor, in the evolution of the mineral industry.

A growing vertical integration can be seen not only in chromite production but also in the case of manganese, copper, and many other minerals. Several of the large steel companies receive over 80 percent of their iron ore from mines in which they have a financial interest. In the case of aluminum, metal producers obtain almost all of their bauxite ore from their own properties. Japanese mineral consumers have ranged the world in their search for mineral properties and have invested heavily in mineral development in many countries.

Captive mining offers many attractions to industrial countries. Among other benefits, it helps stabilize manufacturing costs in mineral consuming industries and, although it may sometimes create problems for small producers, it frequently increases general profitability in the minerals industry. Foreign investment in minerals production can also make a significant contribution to the economies of developing countries.

It is clear, however, that the interests of an international mining corporation and its host country can sometimes diverge, and that there can be quite legitimate disagreements about the pace and style of mineral development. These disagreements may lead producing countries to limit the use of their resources or demand larger payments from the producing company. For this reason, international companies carefully consider the political as well as the geographical characteristics of a country in their decision to develop a mineral area. This point is explored further in chapter 8.

In the case of chromium a unique and important political event has influenced the geography of mining and trade in recent years. This was the unilateral declaration of independence by Rhodesia, and the decision of first the British government and then the United Nations to place an embargo upon the country's exports. Until 1967, Rhodesia was among the leading producers of chromite. In the previous year it produced over 500,000 tons and was the third largest producer in the world. The country's reserves of ore are enormous; in one estimate they stand at 23 percent of the world total, second only to those of South Africa (which has 75 percent of the global figure).

Following the imposition of the United Nations' embargo, the output of chromite in Rhodesia fell—to an estimated 363,000 tons in 1970—while world demand has steadily increased. The exact performance of the industry is uncertain. Production for domestic stockpile and exports via South Africa have continued. The increased shipments of chromite from South Africa, from 700,000 tons in 1967 to nearly a million tons in 1970, could well have included some Rhodesian ore. However, once the United States had officially endorsed the United Nations' embargo in 1968 and had temporarily cut off supplies from its third most important source of chromite, representing about one-fifth of the country's chromite imports, a major shift occurred in the flow of Rhodesian ore.

The major beneficiary of the United Nations' decision was almost certainly the U.S.S.R. By 1970 it had become the largest source of chromite for the United States market and had usurped the traditional role of South Africa. Of American imports of chromite ore in 1970, 33 percent (1,275,000 tons) came from the U.S.S.R., 29 percent from South Africa, and 18 percent from Turkey. The relative importance of (high-grade) Soviet imports was even greater on the basis of their value, representing 43 percent of American chromite imports compared with 23 percent from Turkey and 15 percent from South Africa. Partly in response to this trend, and partly in response to the steadily rising price of chromite in a disrupted market—South African quoted prices rose from $18.70–$21.16 to $24.60–$26.57 per ton during 1970—the United States Congress defied the United Nations' ban in 1971 and permitted imports from Rhodesia once again. However, although there has been less disruption of mining activities than many people had expected and hoped, there can be little doubt that the prolonged uncertainty over Rhodesia's international political status has occasioned something more than a temporary shift in world chromite production and trade. Certainly, large-scale risk capital is unlikely to be available for the expansion of the mining industry there until a settlement of some sort is reached.

MOLYBDENUM AND VANADIUM (two extreme cases of isolated occurrence, in which by-product recovery is very important) • While manganese serves partly as a "scavenger" in steelmaking, molybdenum and vanadium, used in much smaller quantities, play the role of "vitamins." Molybdenum improves steel's hardening qualities and resistance to shock. It is used in combination with other alloying elements in high-speed cutting tools, propeller shafts, turbine rotors, armor-piercing projectiles, and the like. Vanadium is added to some grades of alloy steels to improve their heat-treating characteristics, toughness, and mechanical properties. It is used in steels for making springs, tools, high-speed parts, and permanent magnets.

Both minerals are of rare occurrence, for in each case there is only one known ore body of any significance: molybdenum at Climax, high in the mountains of Colorado; vanadium at Mina Ragra, high in the Andes of Peru. In each case, the restricted nature of the supply stimulated a broad search for new sources. No new deposits have been found, but techniques have been developed which make it economically practical to recover as by-products the minor amounts of molybdenum and vanadium that occur in the ores of other metals.

This is by-product production, and it is a step towards making more complete use of all the material in an ore. In the case of molybdenum, over one-fifth of an estimated world production of 150,000 tons of molybdenite (see table 8) came from the Climax mine. A second mine at Henderson, near Climax, is under development for production in the middle 1970s, and there are also small mines in Canada and Australia. However, an increasing proportion of the metal in recent years has come from the copper mines in the western United States and in Chile. Here the ore is mined for copper, and all the basic costs of mining and milling can be charged against the copper content. The ore nevertheless contains minor amounts of other elements such as molybdenum (the ores of one by-product producer are reported to contain about 0.04 percent molybdenite as compared with 0.6 percent at Climax). This material can be either thrown away or recovered; the choice depends upon the cost of recovering it from the copper concentrate and the value of the metal on the market. With world demand tripling over the past twenty years, and with some countries increasing their needs at an even faster rate—Japan's consumption during the 1960s grew at an annual average rate of 15 percent—it is not surprising that an increasing number of copper producers have elected also to become by-product producers of molybdenum.

In a similar way, vanadium—which is actually more abundant in the earth's crust than copper—is recovered as a by-product of iron ore mining in South Africa, of uranium mining in the Four Corners area of the Colorado Plateau, and of phosphorus production in Idaho (table 9). But, in contrast to molybdenum, the quantities available have become so large that they have taken over the whole of the world market and the one vanadium mine, in Peru, has been closed.

TABLE 8		*Thousand tons*	*% of world*
Major producers of	U.S.A.	84	56
molybdenite, 1970	Canada	27	18
	U.S.S.R.*	12	8
	Chile	10	7
	China	3	2
	Total	136	91
	World	150	100

Source: Institute of Geological Sciences (22, p. 215).
 * Estimate based on 1969 figure.

TABLE 9 | | | *Tons* | *% of world* |
|---|---|---|---|
| **Major producers of** | South Africa | 7,347 | 49 |
| **vanadium, 1970** | U.S.A. | 4,825 | 32 |
| | Finland | 1,315 | 9 |
| | Norway | 980 | 7 |
| | Total | 14,467 | 97 |
| | World | 14,921 | 100 |

Source: U.S. Bureau of Mines (10, p. 1167).

There is a persistent tendency for the by-product producers to make available more vanadium than steel producers and other industrial consumers need or can use.

As this would suggest, a reliance on by-product production has one serious disadvantage: the amount of a metal that is available sometimes bears little relation to the amount needed, and supply does not respond to changes in demand. The supply of molybdenum depends to a large extent on the demand for copper. The source is reliable only so long as the demand for the major product remains high. In the case of molybdenum, it is fortunate that the output of the Climax mine (and shortly the Henderson mine) acts as a balancing force, although the situation is not without risk to the owners, American Metal Climax, Inc. (AMAX); if the demand for copper were to increase significantly, the production of by-product molybdenum could also increase, and this might tend to squeeze that part of the market currently being supplied by mined production. Conversely, of course, AMAX reaps the reward when molybdenum demand is relatively high (in relation to copper) and consumers must fall back upon the non-by-product producer. In the case of vanadium, cutbacks in uranium production could reduce the supply of vanadium and raise its price. Here, however, there are several other alternatives. Some ores are sufficiently rich in vanadium to provide the possibility of producing vanadium as the main product, with uranium as a by-product; and vanadium, as has been seen, can also be recovered as a by-product from other minerals. In any case, the total amount of vanadium used in any year—less than 15,000 tons in 1970—remains small.

THE PATTERN IN REVIEW • Two points can usefully be made in concluding this chapter on the alloying elements. First, it is well to remember again the earlier injunction that the characteristics dealt with in the discussion of individual minerals apply to a greater or lesser degree to other mineral materials. Thus by-products occur in various quantities with many minerals, captive mines are by no means uncommon, and many of the features discussed in succeeding sections can be applied back to the iron ore and steel industries.

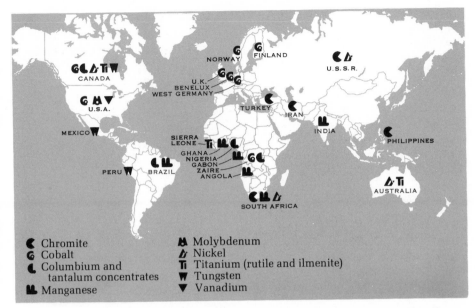

Figure 6. Sources of alloying materials for the United States steel industry, 1970. Although there have been some variations in recent years, such as the decreased importance of Rhodesian chromite, the United States consistently relies upon many countries for its alloying materials. *Source:* Bureau of Mines (10).

Second, in considering different minerals it is wise to make a few crucial comparisons in order to retain perspective. In the case of the alloy minerals, world (1970) production ranges from about 15,000 tons in the case of vanadium; to 150,000 tons in the case of molybdenite; to 621,000 tons of nickel; to almost 6 million tons of chromite; and over 18 million tons of manganese ore. All this is geared largely to supplying raw materials for the world's steel industry, which in 1970 used nearly 420 million tons of iron contained in ore (766 million tons of actual ore) to produce 593 million tons of steel.

It can be seen that in the production of a particular piece of alloy steel many raw materials from a variety of distant places are needed (figure 6). Iron ore from perhaps Labrador or Chile, coking coal from West Virginia or Pennsylvania, and limestone from Michigan are the major constituents in the American case. Of the alloying elements, the manganese may have come from Brazil or from India, the nickel probably from Canada, the chromium from South Africa or the Philippines, the molybdenum from Colorado, and the vanadium as a by-product of some uranium operation in the Four Corners area of the Colorado Plateau.

These are by no means the only raw materials used in the manufacture of steel. There are the refractory bricks, possibly including chromite from the U.S.S.R., which go into the lining of the furnaces; the fluorspar from Illinois or Mexico, which is used as a fluxing material; and a great many other raw materials all of which make their contribution to the manufacture of steel. For that matter, the list of alloying elements, which run the gamut from "a" for aluminum to "z" for zirconium, is by no means exhausted. A single automobile may contain up to eighty different alloy steels. Maintaining a smooth and adequate flow of all these raw materials for the steel industry is undoubtedly one of the biggest and most complex logistical problems in the world.

5 THE BASE METALS: in which the metals are first discussed individually, and then examined together for a consideration of some aspects of the relationship between government and the mineral industry

THE BASE metals have much in common with the ferroalloy minerals from the viewpoint of mining and geology but they present an entirely different economic picture. Although the ferroalloys, such as nickel, chrome, and vanadium, have uses outside the steel industry, the bulk of their production is absorbed by steelmaking. Consequently, the steel industry—with 90 percent of the world market for all metals—is the dominating force in the economics of the ferroalloy group.

The base metals, although they are used to some extent as ferroalloys, derive their major markets from their own particular physical and chemical characteristics. These are the metals that the ancient alchemists tried to convert into gold or silver—usually they include copper, lead, tin, and perhaps mercury—hence the term "base." Today zinc is included in the group, partly because many mines produce zinc along with lead. These are the traditional metals as opposed to newcomers like aluminum, magnesium, and titanium. Each has some special and somewhat unique property which has reserved a place for it in world industry.

Deposits known to the Romans are still being mined, although the bulk of the world's supply currently comes from ores discovered during this century of much expanded demand. Today, in spite of decades of increasing use, there is no medium-term shortage of any of these materials and, in fact, from time to time there has been a large surplus of both reserves and capacity. Estimates of how long this situation will prevail, however, vary from metal to metal. With their long history of production, the base metals illustrate more clearly than most other mineral commodities the interplay among various natural, economic, political, and technological forces which tend automatically to compensate for one another and to assure a continuing supply.

COPPER (in which the concept of resources is examined) • Because it is occasionally found in the native state, copper was one of the first metals worked by man. It is a soft metal, readily shaped with primitive tools, and sometime after 6000 B.C. became the basis for the copper age. Later, about 4,000 years ago when man had learned to alloy his copper with small amounts of tin—which occurred in many of the localities mined for copper—the copper age gave way to the bronze age.

Europe and the Middle East, where copper and bronze came into early use, have many copper deposits, relatively small by today's standards but adequate to supply the limited demand for metal for the tools, utensils, and ornamental work of a preindustrial age. The island of Cyprus, from which the word copper is derived, was a major source of copper to the Romans and is still an important copper mining area; the Erzgebirge, or Ore Mountains, on the border between East Germany and Czechoslovakia, contain deposits of copper and tin in close proximity and are thought to have provided raw materials for the bronze age; Cornwall, in southwest England, whose copper and tin mines were known to the Phoenicians, continued to supply a significant part of the world market for these metals as recently as a hundred years ago.

But the demand for copper has increased far beyond the limits of these deposits. During most of the industrial age copper has been second only to iron as the most widely used metal, and only recently has this position been taken over by aluminum, which had a 1970 output of 9.7 million tons of metal compared with copper's 6.2 million tons. Nevertheless, copper continues as one of the major metals, primarily because of its high electrical and thermal conductivity and its resistance to corrosion.

Approximately one-half of copper supplies is used for electrical applications. Uses in the building industry are also important, as copper metal (in the form of wire, sheets, or pipe), as bronze (alloyed with tin) or as brass (alloyed with zinc). Although many of the traditional markets for copper in such things as electricity transmission lines, pipes, and fixtures are today being shared with newer and cheaper substitutes, primarily aluminum and plastics, the demand for all materials has been increasing at such a rate that worldwide copper production has continued its steady growth. Perhaps somewhat to the surprise of those who worry about the possible exhaustion of mineral supplies, known copper reserves are also at an all-time high.

Although there are thousands of copper deposits throughout the world, the bulk of copper-in-ore comes from only a few areas. Of the 1970 world output, which approached 6 million tons (table 10), nearly 1.1 million tons (18 percent) came from a small area spanning the boundary between Zambia and the Katanga Province of the Republic of Zaire. Some 1.6 million tons came from a scatter of mines in the western United States—with Arizona accounting for over 50 percent of the total. Chile and Canada (mainly Ontario and Quebec) between them accounted for a further 1.3 million tons of production. And these few areas, plus the 0.6 million-ton output of the U.S.S.R., provided over 75 percent of the world's copper. The major part of this ore is produced by a small number of companies, which in most cases have interests and operations in several countries. No other major metal shows quite this degree of concentration in both production location and producers.

TABLE 10		Thousand tons	% of world
Major producers	(a) Mined copper ore (metal content):		
of copper, 1970	U.S.A.	1,560	26
	Chile	686	12
	Zambia	684	11
	Canada	613	10
	U.S.S.R.	571	10
	Zaire	386	6
	Peru	212	4
	Total	4,712	79
	World	5,959	100
	(b) Refined copper:		
	U.S.A.	1,489	24
	Japan	705	11
	Zambia	684	11
	Chile	648	10
	U.S.S.R.	571	9
	Canada	493	8
	Zaire	385	6
	Total	4,975	79
	World	6,226	100

Source: U.S. Bureau of Mines (10, pp. 498, 499).

Plate 4. Papua, New Guinea. The open-cut copper mine operated by Bougainville Copper Pty. on Bougainville Island came into production during April 1972 and by the end of 1973 was producing at the rate of 120,000 tons of contained copper in concentrate. The photograph shows the pit area, shortly before commissioning, divided and encircled by 80-ft.-wide mine haul roads. Accommodation camp and mine service areas are at the bottom left. (Courtesy RTZ [Rio Tinto Zinc].)

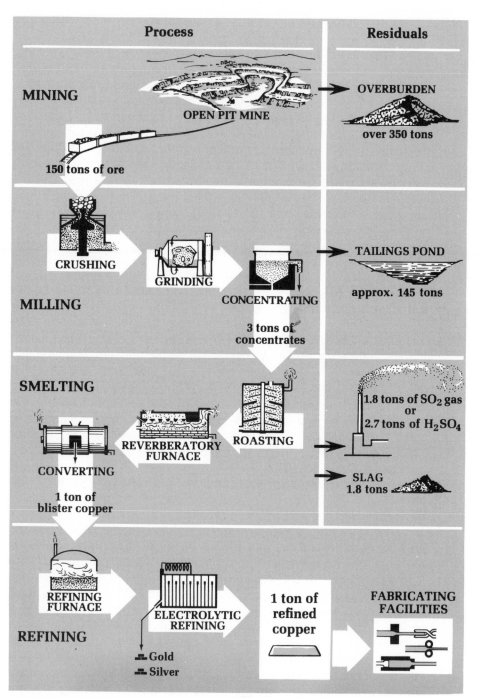

Figure 7. Principal stages in converting copper ore into the finished product. As related in chapter 8, enormous environmental problems are posed by the large amount of tailings produced at the milling and concentration stages, and by the waste gases released in smelting and refining. Tonnage of residuals is based upon experience in the southwestern United States where ores containing only about 0.6 percent copper are now mined.

Copper is produced through a series of complex milling, smelting, refining, and fabricating processes (figure 7). In contrast with the iron and steel industry, the location of copper smelting and refining operations has tended to shift away from the markets for metal and sources of fuel towards the locations of mining as the proportion of metal to waste in copper ores has fallen. For example, South Wales, and in particular the Lower Swansea Valley, was once the largest center of copper smelting in the world—but today it smelts no ore at all. In contrast, the major production centers of copper ore are now also the chief locations of copper refining—the United States, Zambia, Chile, the U.S.S.R., Canada, and Zaire. Only Japan, relying heavily upon higher-grade imported ores from South America and Central Africa, has developed a large smelting industry—in 1970 second only to that of the United States—without at the same time boasting a substantial level of domestic copper mining. In 1970 Japanese production of copper-in-ore was a mere 124,000 tons, compared with its production of 705,000 tons of refined copper.

THE CONCEPT OF RESOURCES IN MINERAL SUPPLY • Confidence concerning the future supply of copper stems not only from the fact that existing mines still have large reserves, but also from statistical evidence that indicates a continued expansion of the world's reserves of this important mineral. Here the long history of copper production and the relatively good records provided by the limited number of major producers and producing areas make possible more comprehensive studies of long-term supply than can be carried out for most mineral commodities. They bear out the principle that the mineral resources of the earth are by no means restricted to what has been proved to exist, and that man will continue to find new materials as he needs them.

At this point it is necessary to be aware of the fact that there is a great deal of variability or flexibility in what constitutes a mineral resource. For many decades the "miner's concept," embracing only that material known to exist and that could be mined under existing conditions, has been accepted as a standard measure. But we have already seen, for example in the discussion of iron ore, that new deposits continue to be discovered; that the conditions under which deposits are developed change over time; and that material such as taconite, which twenty years ago was not seriously considered as a source of iron, can enter the supply picture and lead to significant changes in what is considered to be a usable mineral resource. A more objective evaluation must therefore take account of all those materials that might be available over time. In assessing supply on this broader plane, the need is for terms of reference that will not only satisfy the miner through identifying what is known and can be produced today under specified conditions, but also satisfy the broader requirements and interests of society through taking into account what is likely to be discovered and may be susceptible to production over time under varying conditions.

How can evaluations and resource statements deal with that vast amount of material which has yet to be discovered, is not exploitable at today's costs and with today's techniques, but nevertheless makes up the greater part of future mineral supply? One answer suggested by Resources for the Future and others involves use of the terms (1) *reserves,* for those ore bodies that are judged to be suitable for profitable exploitation under existing economic, technological, and political conditions—essentially, the material that the miner would consider; (2) *resources,* for material that can be expected to become a part of the reserve category during the foreseeable future through discovery or through changes in economic, technological, or political conditions; and (3) *resource base,* for the total amount of metal in the earth. Figure 8 tabulates the reserve-resource concepts just described. (42, p. 298)

More precise classifications do exist, particularly on the level of reserves, which can be broken down into "present reserves" and "potential reserves"; these in turn can be broken down, the present reserves into "measured and inferred," and potential reserves into "marginal and submarginal." (See refs. 2, pp. 1 ff; 27, pp. 236–37.) Such classifications as these may be useful if one is attempting to attach numbers to available material, but for our purpose, which is to provide a broad picture of minerals and mineral supply, too much statistical data might mislead rather than enlighten. The terms *reserves, resources,* and the *resource base,* as defined, have the advantage of

| TERMS | ASPECTS | | |
	Occurrence	Economic	Technological
RESERVES	Known	**Present cost level**	**Currently feasible**
RESOURCES	Known and unknown	**Any cost level specified**	**Currently feasible and probable future feasibility**
RESOURCE BASE	Known and unknown	**Irrelevant**	**Feasible and infeasible**

Figure 8. A tabulation of reserve-resource terminology. *Source:* Schurr and others (42, p. 298).

covering both the specific and the general and allow for the high degree of flexibility that is known to exist.

To examine how this terminology can serve to identify what is and is not known about the quantities of a particular mineral, it is helpful to turn once again to the case of copper. Beginning with the observation that copper (as one of the elements) is distributed throughout the earth's crust, then all of this copper represents the resource base. How great is the resource base in the case of copper? The simple answer is: very great, for copper or for any other mineral material. But what does this mean? It is possible to estimate the amount of copper in the earth's crust—the resource base—at least in terms which give an order of magnitude. On the basis of extensive sampling of the rocks of the earth's crust, geologists estimate that they contain an average 55 parts per million of copper. Working from this, it is possible to arrive at a figure for the absolute limit to copper supplies if one were to dig up the top mile of the globe and process it. This figure, which is over 600 million times the level of recent annual production of new copper, is obviously of little practical significance, but it does provide a frame of reference.

At the other end of the scale is the most precise resource category, the reserves. Not only is the material in this category known to exist, but records provide reasonably good information on where, in what quantity, and of what grade. There is, of course, some small variation in the quality of this knowledge since the measured component of reserves has been subject to detailed mining surveys and tests, while the inferred reserves are measured only in the light of reasonably reliable geological and other assumptions. These, then, are the materials which are known, and which can be recovered at today's costs and with present technology. They make up the infinitesimal part of the resource base on which the world relies for its mineral supplies today and in the near future.

How large are the U.S. reserves of copper? The answer depends partly on what authority one consults. RFF's study of 1961 (38, p. 453) gave a figure of at least 50 million tons, while a later estimate of the Bureau of Mines (9, p. 536) placed U.S. copper reserves at 85.5 million tons. In contrast, the country's copper resource base, must be some million times these amounts. Why then are these reserves only a fraction of the resources that the earth could ultimately yield?

The major reason is that producers of copper, or any other mineral, are concerned only with that portion of the earth which holds out a reasonable promise of profitable exploitation in the near future. There must be vast amounts of attractive ore in the resources category which it would be technically possible to put a figure on. But to measure this material in sufficient detail for it to be shifted into the reserve category costs considerable sums of money which companies are reluctant to spend unless they have early need of additional reserves.

Exploration and proving costs alone can represent one-third of total production expenses. Since all future values in a market economy are subject to a discount at the going rate of interest on capital, a mining company (which is frequently investing its funds with an opportunity cost of capital of 15 percent, and which is writing off its equipment over a five- to eight-year period) cannot afford to invest funds in proving a reserve which will not be needed for twenty years or more. At a low 5 percent rate of interest, the present value of $100 in twenty years' time is only $35; at 10 percent it is worth $15; and at a 15 percent rate of interest, a mere $6. With future ore valued by the mining industry in this way, it is inevitable that the reserves of some minerals tend to be no more than about fifteen or so years' requirements at expected levels of demand, and that these figures serve more as a working inventory of raw material needs than as a true measure of available resources.

Actually, the reserve figures for most minerals are higher than might be expected on the basis of a fifteen-year time horizon. To a large extent this is due to two factors: the development of new operations in remote areas requires a very high level of long-term investment in service facilities—roads, power, town site, and other necessities—as well as mining and processing facilities; an investing company must know that an ore body will justify these expenditures, not only in the eyes of the mining engineer but also in the eyes of the company accountants and stockholders. Even in continuing operations, a company may prove considerably more ore than it strictly needs to for its own planning purposes because once the sampling and testing equipment is set up it may cost relatively little extra to do additional drilling and sampling; the additional proven reserves always look good on the books and are responsive to government and public concern over reserve levels. The reserve figures also reflect the fact that they normally include a portion that is only "inferred." The size of this portion, which may be substantial, is estimated from specific knowledge of the "proven" reserve and reasonable inferences drawn from general knowledge.

In a real sense, however, the known reserves of copper or any other mineral are a direct reflection of the amount of money that has been spent looking for them. It is partly for this reason that the reserves of minerals in the U.S.S.R. on occasions tend to be somewhat more impressive than those of the market economies. In Russia, the exploration of minerals is financed and carried out within a completely different conceptual and institutional framework. Especially important is the fact that exploration activities are not financed through the same channels as development and production. Exploration money is provided in response to a set of politico-economic objectives—such as the importance of mineral self-sufficiency or the opportunities available to earn hard currencies—which are somewhat different from those of the non-Communist world. Moreover, in the socialist or mixed economies of the developing world the state is sometimes prepared to carry exploration and proving expenditures for minerals in order to support broader national economic goals. Thus, in many cases global reserves are large enough to last substantially longer than the fifteen to twenty years noted earlier.

With future reserves of minerals valued and quantified in these ways, it is inevitable that detailed knowledge of a region's or a country's mineral wealth is much scantier than is sometimes realized—even in countries, such as the United States, that can employ the most modern and elaborate of exploration technology. It is not surprising, also, that major new discoveries of minerals continue to be made, and that the size of mineral reserves continues to be revised upwards as material is shifted from the resource to the reserve category through exploration and development programs. So far the process has worked well, although the grade of the ore that has been incorporated in the reserves of many minerals, including copper, has progressively tended to decrease. However, there are some critics who argue that resource appraisal in the market economies tends to undervalue the future, and that public interest requires the assurance of the longer-term availability of at least certain key minerals. For this reason it becomes acceptable for governments to bear some of the risks of exploration and to afford some assistance in the development process. The new Duval Sierrita copper mine in Arizona was, in fact, partly financed by loans from the United States government, loans that will be repaid by deliveries of refined copper to the national stockpile.

As the mineral industries move to the limits of their existing reserves and then develop new reserves, they are in fact encroaching upon what were previously resources: material being shifted from the unknown to the known through discovery; material being made economically recoverable through lowering the cost of recovery or raising the price; material being made exploitable through advances in technology. Thus, in the United States in recent years, new discoveries in Arizona have provided the reserves of the Mission mine and the Sacaton project near Casa Grande—1970 reserves of 48 million tons assaying 0.95 percent copper; a reduction of mining and processing costs has allowed the use of lower-grade materials in other porphyry copper areas of the Southwest, and has further substantially increased U.S. reserves; new mining, haulage, and treatment techniques have made the whole low-grade porphyry copper development possible, for this material must be handled in large quantities using the most modern methods.

Plate 5. Northeast Transvaal, South Africa. The open-cut copper mine of the Palabora Mining Company, Ltd., operates in conjunction with a concentrator, smelter, and refinery on the same site. The entire complex produces up to 90,000 tons of metallic copper each year in addition to magnetite, sulfuric acid, and vermiculite. (Courtesy RTZ [Rio Tinto Zinc].)

Thus, the border between mineral reserves and resources is continually shifting. The average grade of copper ore mined in the United States has declined from about 3 percent in 1880 to about 2 percent in the 1906–10 period, to 1 percent in the 1941–50 period, to 0.72 percent in 1960, and to 0.59 percent in 1970. So far, in the case of copper this shift has not been accompanied by an increase in copper's real price, that is, a price measured in terms of the general U.S. price level.

If we consider copper as it might have been viewed in 1880, ores of 3 percent or a little less would at that time have been classed as reserves, materials down to 2 percent might have been considered as resources, and almost everything mined today would have been down in the resource base. (The porphyry coppers of the Southwest, which account for the bulk of U.S. current production, were not opened up until early in this century.) Today, in contrast, with the average grade of copper ores less than 0.6 percent copper, the United States has material in the reserve category which runs down to 0.4 percent—but it also has material of a higher grade which is now classed as a resource because of its less favorable nature or location. This trend is not peculiar to the United States. While the high-grade copper ores of Zaire, Zambia, and Chile continue to be exploited, scores of low-grade deposits in porphyry rock are being developed in British Columbia, Iran, Bougainville, and elsewhere. These worldwide developments tend to confirm the view of Samuel G. Lasky, an American geologist, that as the grade of mined copper ore falls so will the size of the mineral's reserves substantially increase. Some of the environmental problems associated with the exploitation of such low-grade resources are raised in chapter 8.

Any attempt to employ precise numbers in the discussion of mineral reserves and resources, therefore, is likely to raise more questions than it seeks to answer. The reserves of copper vary with time and technology, with market shifts and the costs of transport, with price, and with politics. So it is with all minerals. Unsatisfactory though such a situation might appear to those who seek finite answers to resource questions, it is the reality within which an interpretation and understanding of the mineral industry must be made.

LEAD (in which the importance of scrap as a raw material is considered) •
The metals lead and zinc are often considered together because they occur together in many of the world's mining areas. However, the use of lead long preceded that of zinc. With silver, it was recovered from the mines of Laurium, near Athens, as early as 1200 B.C., and was beaten into coinage and ornaments. Later the Romans used this metal, which is soft, easy to work, and melts at a relatively low temperature, to line their baths and to carry water throughout their cities. Roman

water pipes were produced in a number of standard lengths and were made by bending a lead sheet around a rod, thus forming a tube which was sealed with solder or with melted lead. Lead pipes like these, excavated at Pompeii and other Roman cities, are still in relatively good condition. The Roman use of lead, which in Latin is called *plumbum,* has given us the word "plumbing."

As with most metals in the preindustrial age, local deposits of lead were adequate to supply most of the limited local demand. The Laurium mines yielded enough for the Greeks. The Romans, whose demands were greater, took lead (as well as other metals) from southern Spain and Pennine England. Under the pressure of modern demands, many of these mining areas, which were subsequently abandoned, have been reopened to yield more of their wealth in the present century.

Although plumbing is still an important use for lead, especially in the less developed economies, the major uses today are related to the automobile industry. In the United States, the largest quantity goes into storage batteries, which use about 44 percent of all lead consumed; the next largest quantity is for tetraethyl lead, which accounts for somewhat more than 20 percent of consumption and is used in gasoline as an antiknock additive; lead pigments account for about 7 percent; and the remainder of the market is largely for a variety of products including ammunition, cable covering, solder, sheet and pipe, and as a shield against radiation. There has been a considerable shift in the market for lead over the past twenty years as substitutes have made inroads into a number of the traditional uses, cable covering and pigments in particular. These have been offset, however, by the buoyancy and growing size of the automobile market, which has helped to keep the United States a leading consumer and producer of both mined ore and of refined lead (table 11).

The single most important source of lead in the United States is domestic and imported scrap, which in 1970 accounted for 40 percent of the lead in the market. Imports of primary lead accounted for a further 23 percent, and a steadily increasing domestic output of new lead for the remaining 37 percent, some 519,000 tons. Four states accounted for 96 percent of this output. Missouri, which has been the country's major lead producing state throughout this century and is its only source of truly lead ores, accounted for nearly 74 percent of the total. Its output has increased briskly in recent years following the discovery during the late 1950s of a new lead belt, the so-called Viburnum Trend, with reserves of over 25 million tons. The other producing states are Idaho, Utah, and Colorado, where the lead is recovered from ores in which other metals—zinc, silver, copper, and gold—are present in important quantities.

Throughout the late 1950s lead production in the United States

TABLE 11   *Thousand tons*   *% of world*

Major producers of lead, 1970	(a) Mined lead ore (metal content):		
	U.S.A.	519	15
	Australia	450	13
	U.S.S.R.	440	13
	Canada	358	11
	Mexico	177	5
	E.E.C.*	167	5
	Peru	155	5
	Total	2,266	67
	World	3,404	100
	(b) Refined lead:		
	U.S.A.	605	18
	E.E.C.*	441	13
	U.S.S.R.	440	13
	Australia	353	11
	Japan	209	6
	Canada	186	6
	Total	2,234	67
	World	3,300	100

Source: U.S. Bureau of Mines (10, pp. 664, 665).
* Enlarged, as of 1973.

declined erratically in response to a weak market and surplus capacity overseas; and by 1962 the mines produced only 215,000 tons of lead, the lowest domestic production since the turn of the century. To help stabilize the industry, the federal government imposed import quotas for both lead and zinc from late 1958. Encouraged by this and by a generally expanding economy, the lead mining industry in the United States increased its exploration efforts, reopened old mines and developed new ones, with the result that the last decade has seen steadily increasing American lead production.

Elsewhere in the world, Australia, the U.S.S.R., and Canada have emerged as major producers of lead ore. Together with the United States, these countries account for over half the global output. The lead is recovered from its ore by means of smelting in blast furnaces or ore hearths, employing carbon fuels. These yield a bullion containing 97 to 99 percent lead, which can be further refined to remove either the remaining impurities or, in some cases, precious metals such as gold and silver. The bulk-reducing nature of the smelting operations encourages the production of refined lead at or near to the sources of ore. However, there is a substantial international trade in ore and concentrates and, as table 11 shows, the major industrialized countries of the world produce significantly more refined lead than ore. Together, the United States, the countries of the (1973) European

Economic Community, the U.S.S.R., and Japan account for half the world production of refined lead.

SCRAP (a major source of raw material) • The 40 percent or so of the lead consumed in the United States that is termed secondary lead has already passed through a cycle of manufacture and use, and it has been returned for resmelting to plants using scrap as their basic raw material. While domestic mines produced nearly 520,000 tons of new lead in 1970, the secondary plants recovered a total of over 540,000 tons. In Britain, where only 3,000 tons of lead are mined annually and where the economy rests heavily upon lead imports, the dependence upon scrap supplies is even more important—some 56 percent of total consumption.

To understand the source of this secondary material, it is only necessary to consider the major use of lead. As has been mentioned, automobile batteries account for about 44 percent of current U.S. consumption. A battery has a relatively short life; after two or three years the lead in the battery is salvaged. There is very little permanent loss in this particular use and the lead may be recycled and reused many times. However, in the case of the second major use of lead, as tetraethyl lead in fuels, the material is burned up with gasoline and is lost forever. Thus this share of annual consumption, some 23 percent, is nonrecoverable. It is a share likely to decline in the future, however, because of the mounting concern about the longer-term effects of lead inhaled from vehicle exhausts and deposited in body tissue. In the United States, the Environmental Protection Agency has proposed a 60 percent reduction of lead in gasoline by January 1978.

These days, a reassessment of this whole area of the secondary recovery of materials is taking place, especially in the technologically advanced world. The United Nations Conference on the Human Environment, held in Stockholm in 1972, revealed a growing interest in recycling metals, a subject that hitherto has received less attention than its complexity and importance warrant. Scrap is a major source of supply for many materials and metals. In addition to accounting for about 40 percent of U.S. lead consumption, it contributes some 25 percent of annual copper consumption, 22 percent of zinc consumption (most zinc uses are nonrecoverable), and supplies almost half of the ferrous raw material going into the making of steel. In 1970, when the U.S. steel industry produced 119 million tons of steel, it consumed 82 million tons of pig iron and 66 million tons of scrap metal. A relatively new metal like aluminum has not had time to build up large stocks of recycled material, although by 1970 over 700,000 tons of aluminum—more than 17 percent of consumption—were recovered. In due course, the contribution of scrap aluminum to annual consumption can be expected to increase considerably above its present level.

As the stock of metal-in-use builds up over the years, it will un-doubtedly become an increasingly important factor in long-range mineral supply. In some countries, as domestic resources are gradually depleted or become relatively more expensive, secondary metal is likely to become the principal domestic resource for a number of metal industries. Already this is the case with the British lead industry, as we have seen. In the future, scrap supplies will also become more important as they reduce the demands made upon the raw material industries and help to reduce the growing dependence of many in-dustrial nations upon foreign mineral sources, for they are materials the industrialized countries already own.

This stock of scrap is made up of two principal elements. The figures quoted earlier for lead, zinc, copper, and aluminum refer to "old" scrap rather than "new" scrap. So-called new scrap is material salvaged at intermediate stages of metal working and metal processing and is in the form of croppings, clippings, trimmings, punchings, dis-carded rods and plates, and the like. Sometimes a distinction is drawn between the "home" or "works" scrap, produced in the metal-making plant, and "process" scrap, produced in the engineering or product manufacturing plant. Over 60 percent of the 66 million tons of scrap used by the U.S. steel industry in 1970 was in this new scrap category.

Old scrap, on the other hand, is material that has been manu-factured, sold to consumers, used, discarded, and is now being re-claimed and salvaged. Automobile graveyards yield large amounts of such scrap. In recent years, with sophisticated and mechanized methods of handling old cars, a substantial percentage of the ma-terials they contain is recovered, and the scrap is delivered to the steel and other metal industries in a more acceptable form than in the past. In contrast, articles such as large oil drums are too expensive to col-lect for the small amount of metal they can yield. They serve to remind us that the value of the metal, plus the cost of scrap collection and transport, continue to dictate the amount that is economic to recycle.

Enthusiasm for recycling materials in modern societies needs, therefore, to be tempered by the realization that the more efficient and sophisticated the scrap metal industries become, the greater is the importance of scrap economics. The scrap merchant of yesterday, with cart and yard, pursued a trade that was as much a way of life as a market-oriented industry; the capital investment was small and the pattern of activity highly variable. Increasingly he has been replaced by a capital-intensive activity that will only accept and process scrap which can yield an adequate return upon the investment involved. If the modern scrap industry does not adequately serve the total needs of a society—by failing to clear scrap quickly enough to meet aesthetic preferences, or by failing to collect a wide enough range of waste materials to satisfy the needs of conscience—then it will be necessary for governments to exert their influence and ensure that the public's environmental or conservation goals can be achieved.

An example of an attempt in this direction can be found in the United States where, under the National Environmental Policy Act of 1969, a Council on Environmental Quality has been created in the Executive Office of the President. An early report to Congress has suggested the creation of a bounty system on old automobiles (payable to the processor, wrecker, or owner) in order to reduce the number of cars—currently between 2.5 and 4.5 million out of a total annual retirement of 9 million—that are abandoned each year. Although this advice was rejected, the point must be taken that economic incentives rather than ecological zeal are the most appropriate way to get more used metal back into the production system. One suggestion to this end is that the tax laws on scrap metal should be made more comparable with those on ore. For example, new metal benefits from depletion allowances of 15 or 22 percent, payable to the mining industry; a similar credit to scrap processors, which could be passed on to the consumers of scrap in the form of lower prices, would have an enormous impact upon the economic attractiveness of recycling metals.

ZINC (in which further consideration is given to the importance of the grade of ore, including the lead-zinc ores) • Although some form of zinc was first used in India and China as a component of brass, and the ores of zinc were certainly encountered and used by early metal workers in Europe, the metal is a relative newcomer. It was not until the middle of the eighteenth century that the metal was produced commercially. Zinc eluded early metallurgists because it cannot be smelted by the simple, direct techniques that break down the ores of copper, tin, lead, and iron. Thus zinc, as such, does not have the long history of the traditional base metals. Even today there is a far greater range in the methods of producing zinc than there is for any other common nonferrous metal. The first recorded production of metallic zinc was over a thousand years ago from the Rammelsberg mine in the Harz Mountains of West Germany—a mine still in production and, with the nearby Grund mine, today a modern property accounting for about 66 percent of the lead output and 40 percent of the zinc ore production of that country.

The major modern use of zinc rests on its ability to resist the harmful effects of moisture and gases in the atmosphere. A thin layer of zinc used as a coating protects steel from corrosion. It does this in two ways, first through providing a physical sheath which prevents contact between the metal and the corroding material (even moist air will in time rust most steel), and second through "galvanic" action. Galvani, an eighteenth century Italian scientist, discovered that when two dissimilar metals are in electrical contact with one another in the presence of a conducting liquid, one metal will corrode while protecting the other. In a "galvanic series" with the metals arranged in order of decreasing reactivity, zinc is near the top of the series, and is above iron and steel. Thus a coating of zinc can protect iron and steel against corrosion in the presence of moisture. This process of coating steel is called "galvanizing," and about 40 percent of the zinc currently consumed is used for putting this protective coating on steel. Other major uses are in die castings, brass products, and as zinc oxides for the rubber, paint, and other industries.

Although lead and zinc often occur together in nature, the pattern of zinc supply to the U.S. market—the world's largest—is somewhat different from that for lead. In this case, imports are the single most important source (48 percent in 1970); production from domestic ores comes next (32 percent); and secondary or scrap zinc (20 percent) is considerably less important than is secondary lead. Although much of the world's zinc comes from mines producing other metals, the most important American sources are mines producing primarily zinc located in Tennessee and New York. Because metal mining is generally thought of as "western" industry it comes as somewhat of a surprise to find that over half of the United States' mine production of zinc comes from states east of the Mississippi River.

TABLE 12		Thousand tons	% of world
Major producers of zinc, 1970	(a) Mined zinc ore (metal content):		
	Canada	1,239	23
	U.S.S.R.	610	11
	U.S.A.	484	9
	Australia	484	9
	E.E.C.*	347	6
	Peru	316	6
	Japan	280	5
	Total	3,760	69
	World	5,497	100
	(b) Refined zinc:		
	E.E.C.*	953	19
	U.S.A.	796	16
	Japan	676	14
	U.S.S.R.	610	12
	Canada	418	9
	Australia	260	5
	Total	3,713	75
	World	4,904	100

Source: U.S. Bureau of Mines (10, pp. 1203, 1204).
* Enlarged, as of 1973.

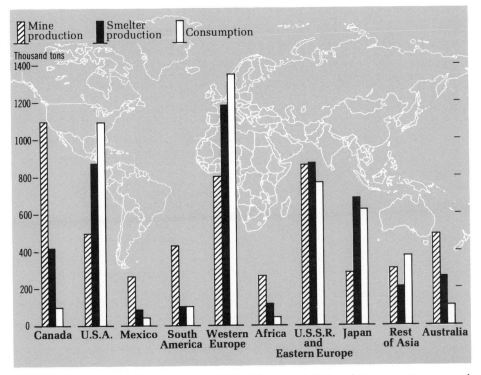

Figure 9. World zinc balance, 1970. The ore deficits of Western Europe and the United States stand out clearly. Japan is unusual insofar as it has a surplus of smelter production at the same time as a deficit of ore. *Source:* Institute of Geological Sciences (22, pp. 380 ff).

In the western states, most of the production now comes from mines producing more than one metal; Colorado is an outstanding producer, while output from the new Missouri lead belt is rapidly increasing.

In 1964, Texas Gulf Sulphur announced a major zinc discovery made at Timmins, Ontario, which led to Canada's current position as the world's leading supplier of this ore (table 12). Also exceeding the American output is the production of the U.S.S.R.; and all the evidence points to Australia taking over as the world's third leading supplier in the early 1970s. These four countries accounted for more than half of world production of zinc ore in 1970. Smelting and refining are a different matter. Major metal markets and hence leading industrial areas play a key role in attracting the location of production (figure 9). Nearly one-fifth of the world's zinc is refined in the countries of the enlarged European Economic Community, and over 60 percent is produced in that economic bloc plus the U.S.A., Japan, and the U.S.S.R. As a consequence, world trade in zinc ores and concentrates is substantial.

For a number of years the supply of zinc on the world market has tended to be in excess of consumption. For this reason, among others, the International Lead and Zinc Study Group meets regularly in Geneva to review the market and resource situation. Paradoxically, this tendency towards surplus zinc capacity and production has coincided with the emergence of a relatively poor reserve position. This cannot be attributed to any fundamental resource deficiency, since zinc is more abundant than copper in the earth. However, the price of zinc is relatively low and offers little financial incentive to explore for new deposits. In addition, zinc is only in part mined independently of other metals.

THE GRADE OF ORE AND ITS IMPACT ON SUPPLY • Earlier, the point was made that over the years the average grade of copper ore mined has been gradually getting lower, but that with improved technology it has been possible to mine the ore and smelt the metal with no increase in real price. It still is true, however, that there are many high-grade ores in the world and that (other things being equal) these ores can be produced more effectively and more economically than lower-grade ores. There are other factors to be considered in metal mining, of course: the location of the ore body can affect the cost of its development; the nature of the ore may make for costly processing; or other economic or perhaps political reasons may tip the scales in favor of developing one deposit rather than another of higher grade. It is these factors, in combination with ore grade, that determine whether it is economic to mine a given ore body, a fact that can be well illustrated with examples from the lead-zinc mining industry.

For the United States as a whole, the average combined grade of all lead-zinc ores in the early 1960s was: zinc 2.6 percent, lead 1.6 percent, copper 0.1 percent, silver 19.6 grams (0.63 fine ounces) per ton, and gold 0.16 grams (0.005 fine ounces) per ton. These values are low, and as many constituents as possible must be recovered if the industry is to be able to continue to operate. Thus, for the same period, 59 percent of the value of the lead-zinc ores came from zinc, 32 percent from lead, and 9 percent from silver, gold, and copper. The ores also contain small and recoverable quantities of antimony, bismuth, and tellurium. From an economic viewpoint each constituent is important. In the case of lead and zinc, then, we go a step beyond by-product production and deal with what can be termed co-products. Co-production exists where more than one metal is present in significant quantities in the ore and where each metal is important and perhaps vital for the profitable operation of the property. Unlike by-product mineral production, a fall in the price of a co-product metal can seriously undermine the economics of a whole mining operation.

The presence of a variety of recoverable minerals, each in rather

small quantities, makes possible the development of important reserves, which could not be developed on the basis of any single constituent. Thus co-production has greatly broadened the ore reserves of
the United States and has greatly extended the life of many mining
districts.

The average grade of lead-zinc ores in the United States is significantly lower than that in other countries producing large quantities
of lead and zinc. Because of these lower grades, which in part are
reflected in higher costs per unit of production, American producers
have been unable to compete easily on a price basis with foreign
producers and in recent years have been supplying less than half of
domestic ore consumption. Once protected by quotas, U.S. production
of zinc ore today shelters behind a modest tariff.

Let us compare the grade of American ore with that of some of
the mines in other countries. Average U.S. production in the 1960s
ran at just over 4 percent combined lead-zinc and less than a fine
ounce (31 grams) of silver per ton. The main foreign producers are
Mexico, Canada, and Australia. Mexican mines run 10 to 13 percent
combined lead-zinc with 5 to 6 ounces of silver per ton. One of the
principal Canadian mines runs about 12 percent combined lead-zinc
and is high in silver. A major Australian producer runs 27 percent
combined lead-zinc and about 7 ounces of silver. Other properties in
the world run even higher. The reserves of the Broken Hill mine in
Rhodesia run 41 percent combined lead-zinc. It should be noted that
in other countries specific producers are quoted while the U.S. figures
represent the average of all producers. Among them are rich lead-zinc
mines and, indeed, averages for the western states are almost double
those of the whole nation. But it is true that in general U.S. reserves
are lower in grade than those of the major foreign producers and that
there are extensive high-grade ores in foreign countries which can
absorb tariffs considerably higher than those currently in force. In
consequence, they can undersell the produce of the American mines
and still make a profit. This may partially explain why zinc reserves
in the United States, which stood at about 30 million tons in 1964 (out
of an estimated world total of 120 million tons), are not particularly
impressive.

Although one can calculate the average grade of the metal ores
mined in a country, a district, or an area, there is in fact no such thing
as an average mine. Each mine has its own peculiarities and characteristics and, perhaps of equal importance, each carries with it the hopes
and faith of those who operate it. But the very wide range of grades
and the very great differences in economic environment indicate why
at any given price some mines are profitable, some marginal, and
some cannot be operated.

This being the case, it follows that some of the large ore reserves of the world could be profitably exploited at prices much lower than those prevailing at present. Figures to illustrate this are difficult to find and are not available for zinc, but Sir Ronald Prain, chairman of the Rhodesian Selection Trust, has provided them for copper. In 1967, at a time when the price of copper in the London market stood exceptionally high at an average of $1,540 per ton, he estimated that 80 percent of the world's copper was being produced at costs of less than $900 per ton, over 50 percent at costs of less than $560 per ton, and about 40 percent at costs of less than $450 per ton. The lowest cost production, incidentally, came from the ore bodies with the lowest metallic content, ores which were mined in massive quantities from open pits using the most modern large-scale technology. These costs apply before deductions for income or other taxes on revenue. They nevertheless confirm the impression that, even with a marked fall in market prices, large quantities of copper would still be made available by the industry. The same would hold true for other minerals.

TIN (in which mineral production in the less developed countries is discussed in relation to the pattern of world mineral supply) • Tin has been used for centuries in the production of ornaments, weapons, and utensils. Although it is by no means as common as the other base metals, it was found in small quantities, often in close physical relationship with copper, in mines spread across Europe. Thus the alloying of these two metals to make bronze was a reasonable and logical step for our forebears in the development of better materials. Since bronze is stronger, harder, and more resistant than either of the metals that go into its making, the Bronze Age marked a great advance in which man learned much about the use and processing of metals.

Until the Industrial Revolution, consumption of tin was surpassed only by that of iron, copper, and lead. Today it has been outstripped by a number of other metals: aluminum, zinc, and some of the ferroalloys such as nickel, manganese, and chrome (although these may not all be processed through to the pure metal stage). The mines of Cornwall in the southwest of England—for centuries the major tin-producing area of the world—were still extremely important a hundred years ago. However, they became completely inadequate to cope alone with the expanding demand of the present century. With their eclipse, stimulus was provided for the development of new properties in many parts of the world, which have taken over the task of meeting man's growing requirements for tin.

Some of the knights in thirteenth-century Bohemia wore tin-plated armor; but they were well in advance of their time, for the widespread use of tin for coating other metals springs from the last century. Today tin plate is the major use of tin, and tin cans are the major use of tin plate. In the plating process a protective coating of tin is placed on a mild carbon steel sheet either by dipping the steel in a bath of molten tin or, more commonly, by electroplating. The new product has both the strength of steel and the corrosion resistance of tin. Steel alone in this form would rust, whereas tin would be too soft and costly. Other major uses are as solder, in which tin is alloyed with lead, and as bronze or brass, in which tin is alloyed with copper. The amount of tin used in the United States, the largest market, is not great. Some 75,000 tons were consumed in 1970, of which 28 percent was old scrap. However, because there are no important domestic deposits, all new supplies are imported. Western Europe and Japan are in a similar position; their demands greatly exceed their relatively small production.

In tin supply, much more than in the other base metals discussed earlier, there is a strong contrast between the geography of demand and the geography of production. Among the major consuming countries, only the U.S.S.R. has a significant domestic production, the third largest in the world. The other major producers are Malaysia, with nearly one-third of the world total, Bolivia, Thailand, China, and Indonesia (table 13). Thus, the western industrial countries are wholly dependent upon outside sources for their tin supplies. The major Communist countries, on the other hand, are not only important producers of tin but in recent years they have had a surplus to export.

TABLE 13		Thousand tons	% of world
Major producers of tin, 1970	(a) Mined tin ore (metal content):		
	Malaysia	74	32
	Bolivia	29	13
	U.S.S.R.	27	12
	Thailand	21	9
	China	20	9
	Indonesia	19	8
	Total	190	83
	World	230	100
	(b) Refined tin:		
	Malaysia	92	41
	E.E.C.*	35	15
	of which:		
	Britain	22	10
	U.S.S.R.	27	12
	Thailand	22	10
	China	20	9
	Total	196	87
	World	226	100

Source: U.S. Bureau of Mines (10, pp. 1101, 1102).
* Enlarged, as of 1973.

In some measure this is a quirk of geology; but it also reflects important differences in the political economy of resource exploration, noted earlier.

At one time much of the tin that was mined in the developing world was transported to Western Europe for refining, and the countries of the enlarged European Economic Community still produce 15 percent of the world output of refined tin, most of it in Britain. However, as with many other metals, for both economic and political reasons there has been a strong tendency during the last few decades for these operations to shift back towards the sources of tin. Thus Malaysia and Thailand together accounted for over half the world production in 1970. An increasing part of international trade in tin is in the refined product rather than the original ore or concentrate.

Over the past fifty years this trade has called for some degree of international supervision. The problem is simple to explain. Because of the relatively small amounts of tin required in proportion to other materials in tin-bearing manufactures, the demand for tin is not price sensitive. Consumption, in other words, does not rise readily in response to a fall in price. Likewise, the large investments required for new production facilities, and the time involved in bringing these into operation, make for a somewhat inelastic supply. In the absence of vertical integration between the producing and the consuming industries, these conditions tend to aggravate fluctuations in the market price for tin, and they have posed major problems, especially for those countries which rely heavily upon the metal for a large part of their foreign exchange earnings.

The response of the industry from 1921 onwards has been to seek a greater stability of prices, through restriction of production and management of stocks, when normal market responses are not fast enough to check violent fluctuations in the price of tin. Designed to help stabilize producer revenue, these measures have also tended to support tin prices and so have prevented the elimination of inefficient, high-cost producers from the industry (47, p. 39). Since World War II, under the auspices of the International Tin Council in London, a series of International Tin Agreements setting production quotas have been signed between the non-Communist producing countries and most of the principal consuming countries in the western world. The United States and West Germany are not members, although they have attended as observers along with the U.S.S.R. The fourth of these Agreements runs from 1971 to 1976. An industry buffer stock of 20,000 tons is managed by the International Tin Council's Buffer Stock Manager in the London market and is supplied by compulsory contributions from the producing countries. The Manager intervenes in the market whenever prices move outside agreed base or ceiling levels. The effectiveness of this institution, which, lacking

U.S. membership, had to work alongside another buffer stock, the United States government stockpile, is discussed in the section of this chapter dealing with the role of government in the base metal industries.

MINERAL PRODUCTION IN DEVELOPING COUNTRIES • A growing proportion of the mineral production of the world is coming from countries which, being in the early stages of industrialization, would like to use mineral production and exports as a means of stimulating and financing economic development. By the middle 1960s the minerals and base metal exports of developing countries represented some 12 percent of all their primary commodity earnings (compared with 36 percent from fuel exports, chiefly oil); and these exports were increasing at a much faster rate than trade in agricultural produce. Among the minerals and base metal exports, the most important foreign exchange earner was copper (with one-third of the total), followed by iron ore (19 percent) and tin (13 percent). Especially in the case of tin, this trade poses certain difficulties or potential difficulties for both producers and consumers.

On the consumer side, industrial nations require significant amounts of tin, which must be imported mainly from Southeast Asia and Bolivia. Since in the past such sources have proved to be somewhat vulnerable to military or political disruption, and since the tin reserves are limited (partly because exploration is limited), there has been a considerable effort to cut down on the use of tin. Substitutes are being employed in many traditional uses, secondary tin is recovered where possible, and techniques are being developed to reduce the amount of tin used in tin-plating. Here, then, the aim has been to cut back the use of this metal; and over the years, to take one outstanding example, U.S. consumption of tin, has actually decreased somewhat.

On the supply side, the biggest source area is the narrow metallogenic belt running from south China down through Thailand and Burma, the length of Malaysia, and ending in the Indonesian islands south of Singapore. The deposits here are mainly alluvial concentrations in sand and gravel, and much of the mining in this area is done with dredges—large, floating, self-contained digging and treatment units, which dig up sand from more than 100 feet (30 meters) beneath the surface, remove the heavy tin minerals, and discard the sand as waste. The other major source is high in the mountains of Bolivia, where mining is underground.

The production of tin is extremely important to the economies of the producing areas. In Indonesia tin normally accounts for about 5 percent of the value of exports from the country, but to the few small islands just south of Singapore tin production is a major activity. In

Malaysia, the major tin-producing region in the world, tin normally accounts for about 20 percent of the value of exports and is one of the country's largest industries.

If tin production is important in Indonesia and Malaysia, it is essential to the economy of Bolivia, where tin accounts for nearly half of the value of exports. This creates a complex situation on a world supply level, for the tin deposits of Bolivia are quite different from those of Southeast Asia and are much more expensive to exploit. Underground mining costs are high; transportation costs are high; and the industry has been plagued by labor troubles. In fact, during periods of relatively low prices, Bolivian tin costs more to produce than it can command in the market; but since it is so important a part of the country's economy, and since the miners are a powerful group, the government has supported the industry with various subsidies.

Any disruption in the market for tin or any serious fluctuation in the price can have extreme repercussions on the total economy in each of these countries, and particularly on the economy of that section of the country which is dependent upon tin. A major downward fluctuation in price can cause considerable trouble. In the case of a country like Bolivia, it has led in the past to starvation, riots, and even changes in government. On the one hand, then, there are consumers who are anxious to cut down on consumption, and, on the other, producers who rely on this market.

This somewhat extreme example highlights one of the crucial problems of mineral development: how to integrate the mineral production of the less developed countries into the mineral supply pattern of the industrial world in such a way that mineral development makes a real contribution both to continuing world supply and to the economic development of the host country. Since industrial countries need minerals and developing countries need foreign exchange and investment capital, this might seem a simple enough matter; but at times the economic and political problems involved make equitable solutions very difficult to find.

Four areas of conflict stand out in particular. The first concerns the international market economy and the value it places upon mineral raw materials. Quite apart from the fluctuations in their worth through time—in the short run with shifts in supply and demand, and in the longer term with changes in the terms of trade—the fact remains that the value of these materials stands quite low in relation to the cost of the final manufactured products of which they eventually form a part. Small increases in mineral prices would make relatively little difference to the cost of production in the advanced industrial economies, yet they would make an enormous contribution to the needs of the developing world. The United Nations Conference on Trade and Development has sought to exert some pressure upon the world market system to the advantage of the poorer nations, but with only moderate success to date. It took the global scarcity of most raw materials in 1973 to generate a decisive increase in their real market values; yet how long these prices can be sustained remains a very open question.

A second area of conflict relates to the allocation of rewards within the mineral exploitation business. Indisputably, rewards are due to the host country for the sacrifice of its nonrenewable resources and for the labor which it frequently contributes in abundance. Equally clearly, rewards are also due to the industrialized nations who supply capital, take risks, offer high-level technological skills, provide management, and exploit their market knowledge. But how the total rewards should be divided between these several claimants is clearly a matter for vigorous debate.

Third is the related and progressively more important area of disagreement concerned with ownership and control of the actual mining operations. There is clearly a growing feeling in some parts of the developing world that the (traditional) ownership of mineral resources by foreign corporations is not in the national interest, since their objectives and priorities cannot possibly coincide with the objectives and priorities of the host country. This is partly exemplified by the fourth area of disagreement, which relates to the location of beneficiating, smelting, and refining facilities. Historically, these were often in the industrialized countries where there were not only the necessary labor skills and technological back-up facilities, but also fewer risks involved in a major capital investment. As part of their efforts to increase the value of their exports, many developing countries have been insisting upon the location of at least some of these facilities near to the mineral sources. It is the intention of the Bolivian government, for example, that all that country's tin should eventually be smelted before export, and under government decrees all producers must now offer their tin concentrates first to the state smelting enterprise.

In a recent RFF study of foreign investment in the petroleum and mineral industries, the point is made that the very nature of resource exploitation arrangements between the developed and the developing world tends to produce conflict. However, as Mikesell notes in that study:

While conflict is unavoidable, so also is accommodation and cooperation if the parties are to promote their common interest. Rational behavior requires the players in the game to seek joint maximizing solutions in which the size of the pie is not reduced by the scramble over the portions. (32, p. 55)

THE BASE METALS AND GOVERNMENT • The fact that mineral raw materials are essential to the industrial well-being of a country has led to a belief in some quarters that a country must be able to supply a significant part of its mineral requirements from its own resources. Once again we return to the broad theme of self-sufficiency discussed in chapter 3 in the case if iron ore. The Soviet Union has opted for maximum self-sufficiency, as we have seen. The various policy alternatives have led to a great deal of controversy in the United States, the largest market for minerals, for they bear on defense or strategic considerations as well as economic factors. The country has as yet been unable to decide upon a consistent policy as to how these factors should be weighed and evaluated. Let us consider the United States' case further.

Traditionally, governments in many market economies have provided some protection to industry, particularly in the case of so-called infant industries, which need a certain amount of help in establishing themselves before they can operate without assistance. The United States government has assisted the mineral industry in a variety of ways to help in the establishment or early development of new mining properties. This was true, for example, in the case of some copper properties developed during and immediately after the Korean War, and more recently during the late 1960s when government loans assisted in the development of the Duval Sierrita copper mine in Arizona.

However, there also is pressure from the industry, from regional authorities, and others to protect mines toward the end as well as at the beginning of their lives; thus the government provides assistance in one way or another for marginal mining properties that could not be kept in operation successfully without some form of subsidy. The small lead and zinc mine assistance program, which was terminated in 1969, fell into this category. In cases such as this, the avowed objective is the maintenance of domestic supply and reserves, mainly for strategic reasons; however, indirect relief to declining mining localities is also a factor. It is felt that it is necessary to keep the domestic mining industry strong so that the country will have a ready source of these materials if foreign supplies are cut off by military or political action. A significant domestic mineral industry gives considerable protection in such circumstances. But the United States has not addressed itself to these issues in any thorough or systematic way. Its response to a changing degree of mineral self-sufficiency over the last thirty years or so can be demonstrated by the sometimes conflicting measures the government has taken affecting the base metals.

Before World War II, the United States exported significant quantities of copper, lead supplies were about in balance, some 5 percent of zinc requirements was imported, and in the case of tin the country was totally dependent upon imports. In the years immediately following the war and up to the present, the United States has been a significant importer of all of these raw materials. The position with regard to copper is still relatively strong, with production now three times higher than prewar levels. But consumption has risen considerably, and in most postwar years America has been a net importer. In the cases of both lead and zinc, the country gets more of its supply of new metal from foreign than from domestic sources, and in both instances output is only slightly higher than in 1939; in the case of lead it is 27 percent higher, and in the case of zinc it is less than 10 percent higher.

Why has production from domestic mines failed to keep pace with rising demand? One can approach this from different directions and find reasons from each. From the physical point of view, the best reserves of the United States have been used up while very rich reserves still remain to be developed in other parts of the world. Therefore, American ores are lower in grade and frequently more costly to mine and process. Some who argue for more domestic mining find an additional reason in the fact that foreign producers also have low labor costs; but this factor is more than balanced by the greater productivity of American industry and by its nearness to the market.

Recognizing the first point, that many American ore reserves are too low in grade to be competitive, a high level of domestic production can only be maintained through government assistance, and the country must decide if this is justified. Sometimes it is, but it is far from easy to make a reasoned appraisal. For many of the countries that supply mineral raw materials to the U.S. market, mining is a relatively more important part of the economy than it is in the United States. Hence, public policy in those countries tends to favor the stimulation of mining activity. Capital (both domestic and foreign) flows into the mining industry and labor finds work in mining more rewarding than any of the alternatives. Indeed, in such countries the alternatives may be few and relatively unattractive. However, in an advanced industrial nation such as the United States there are attractive alternatives for both capital and labor either in industries other than mining or in the more profitable branches of the mining industry.

Although there has been no consistent agreement or policy on whether a strategic interest requires that a particular level of domestic production or capacity be maintained, the shift to significant base metal imports has led to an almost instinctive adoption of a number of direct and indirect methods of subsidizing otherwise uneconomic mineral production. Originally this was in the name of defense; but more recently some programs have been aimed at keeping mines alive in order to provide employment for people in distressed areas.

It would seem that every conceivable type of public program has been tried in the mining industry, sometimes to stimulate new production, sometimes to protect mining properties which cannot operate successfully without assistance, and sometimes to stabilize world production and prices. The means include tariffs, a variety of forms of subsidy, stockpiling, quotas, barter, tax incentives, and international production agreements. All of these programs involve government agencies in one way or another, and they also involve a degree of governmental control over the industry. Each kind of program has been applied to the base metals, and something of the strength and structure of each branch of the industry can be learned from the degree of control that has been applied.

Copper, being in the strongest position among the base metals, has been able to operate with relatively little public assistance, although in times of "national emergency" the companies and the government have cooperated in the opening up of mineral reserves at an accelerated rate. Thus, on a number of occasions the government has stimulated the development of new copper properties through entering into purchase contracts with some of the major copper-producing companies. Exploration loans amounting to 50 percent of costs have also been granted for qualified properties, and copper companies have been given certain tax concessions to encourage the development of new capacity. These programs, carried out chiefly by the handful of large firms that dominate U.S. copper production, have been notably successful in developing new capacity and sources. At the same time, the industry has been left relatively free of institutional government controls and interference.

Overall, the strategic position of copper supplies for the American economy gives little cause for concern. Domestic capacity and reserves, the importance of secondary metal, and the material which has already been stockpiled give the country a high degree of security. Despite the net imports of both ore and refined metal, therefore, any shortages could easily be alleviated through increased domestic production, some substitution of other materials for copper, and an increased recovery of secondary copper balanced out with stockpiled material.

The impact of the various subsidy programs on the copper industry in the past has been quite different from that on lead and zinc. Because in the case of copper the major domestic producers control—or, at least, used to control—a large part of the available foreign production, particularly in Africa and South America, any stimulus to domestic production inevitably reduced the market for their foreign holdings, which in most cases were rich and highly profitable. It also reduced the companies' freedom in balancing the operations of their various domestic and overseas properties. Historically at least—for the situation has clearly begun to change—this was a case in which the richest and most profitable resources of the non-Communist world were in a single production pool; and the companies sought to develop that pattern which most effectively and economically would supply the market. There was only nominal government intervention. A similar set of relationships also applied broadly to the procurement of iron ore, petroleum, and several other mineral raw materials, although each case exhibits some degree of individuality. These relationships have never applied, however, to those minerals for which American producers do not have significant foreign holdings and for which domestic reserves (considered on an industry-wide basis and accepting variations between individual deposits) are not competitive with those in foreign countries.

The lead-zinc industry is the main example of this case. U.S. producers do not have extensive international holdings, and the country's domestic ore reserves overall are not competitive with those in other parts of the world. Currently the lead-zinc industry is protected by tariffs and, with other extractive industries, has benefited from various tax incentives, including accelerated depreciation and percentage depletion allowances. Of all the mineral producers, the lead-zinc industry—with undoubtedly the strongest case for assistance —has benefited most from government aid.

Lead and zinc went into the strategic stockpile under the initial post-World War II stockpiling program. They went into the auxiliary stockpile under the special program inaugurated by President Eisenhower in 1954. And they went into the supplemental stockpile under the barter program by which the United States government barters surplus agricultural commodities for strategic mineral materials. The peak year for this barter program was 1957, in which over 100,000 tons of lead and almost 200,000 tons of zinc were acquired for the supplemental stockpile. This material all came from foreign sources, but, to the extent that it was taken off the market, it indirectly improved the position of the domestic producers.

Over the years, the stockpiling program has created considerable confusion, since its objectives have been changed frequently. At the present time, the stockpile is being steadily reduced in the case of many minerals, since it contains more material than the government thinks is necessary for national security. Only in the case of copper is the inventory lower than the objective, and in most instances it is very much higher. At the end of 1971, the stockpile of both lead and zinc contained over a million tons and was more than double the established objective (table 14). Much of the surplus in the stockpiles was initially acquired through barter agreements with foreign governments.

A quota system on lead and zinc imports which lasted between 1959 and 1965 proved far from satisfactory. The 1962 Tariff Commission report (45, p. 48) noted that the quotas were discriminatory in their effects, that they favored some concerns while creating difficulties for others, and that they seriously interfered with normal trade

TABLE 14	Mineral	Objective	Actual inventory	1970 consumption
Government strategic	Bauxite	10,643	11,564	15,896
stockpile in the	Chromite	3,362	6,423	1,273
United States, 1971	Copper	703	234	1,438*
(thousand tons)	Lead	481	1,023	1,234
	Manganese	3,360	10,154	2,144
	Molybdenum	0	19	21
	Nickel	0	35	141
	Tin	236	255	54*
	Titanium sponge	30	32	15
	Vanadium	0.5	3	5
	Zinc	508	1,014	1,425

Sources: *Mining Journal Annual Review,* June 1972,
p. 281; U.S. Bureau of Mines (10).
* Primary metal.

relations. All in all, the program for bolstering the domestic industry through trade restrictions was clearly inappropriate to the needs of both the industry and the country. And as United States' trade policy shifted toward freer trade and less restriction, this approach to the protection of the lead-zinc industry was discarded.

One form of government action to assist the industry provides a direct subsidy to small lead-zinc mines. It was intended that this subsidy gradually diminish over a period of years and it has; the assistance seems to be designed to help the mines to go out of operation gradually rather than help them to remain in production. But this program may be indicative of the government's present policy towards mineral development and, in this particular situation, it may be the most reasonable approach. With short-term supplies guaranteed from domestic mines, secondary material and a government stockpile that currently stands well above the minimum levels specified under the various Acts, the United States is in a strategically strong position. Moreover, two of the major sources of imports are Canada and Mexico, both of which are accessible by both land and ocean routes.

So far as the United States is concerned, the tin industry is a quite unusual case in which there is no domestic production and in which no American companies are involved as principal producers. The solution adopted towards strategic problems, therefore, has been to establish and maintain a stockpile of 236,000 tons, compared with the 1970 demand for 54,000 tons of primary tin and 21,000 tons of secondary material. This target was considerably exceeded in the late 1950s, but much of the surplus, acquired through barter agreements, has been gradually sold off by the General Services Administration. Tin is also eligible for up to 50 percent loans on exploration expenditure; but, no loans have in fact been made.

The tin industry also provides an extreme case of international public intervention in the world market under the International Tin Agreements. Producers and consumers meet together quarterly to estimate the demands of the world and to allocate this demand among the producing countries. Countries are given votes on the Tin Council in relation to their production or their consumption of tin. The United States is in a somewhat awkward position in relation to the International Tin Agreements. The Executive branch was originally one of the major supporters of the institution and was active in setting it up. However, the Tin Agreements are aimed at price-fixing and at stabilizing fluctuations in price and production, and Congress has never been willing to approve participation in this particular international commodity agreement. As an "observer," the United States has, however, cooperated closely with the Council and has provided information on American consumption for use in determining production quotas.

The four International Tin Agreements, which have run for successive five-year periods from 1956, provide the only recent example of a successful attempt by an international institution to control the world price and production of a mineral through concerted international action. There can be little doubt that the arrangement has helped to stabilize the price of tin. For example, during the First Agreement from 1956 to 1961, tin prices ranged from $1,792 to $2,464 per ton, whereas during the previous five years the price had fluctuated between $1,585 and $4,536. There have, of course, been times when the machinery appeared somewhat frail. For example, in the late 1950s, when exports from the U.S.S.R. appeared on the market in large quantities, the funds of the Buffer Stock Manager were quickly exhausted and tin prices fell through the agreed "floor." Again, in the late 1960s the manager had to restrict his activities following an extended period of tin shortages during which the ceiling price had ceased to be at all realistic. It is also clear, looking back, that the activities of the Council were significantly assisted by the activities of the United States government. In the period 1962 to 1964, for example, when the world market was characterized by shortages, the Agreement was held only with the release of large quantities of tin (nearly 30,000 tons in 1964 alone) from the American stockpile. Shortages in this same period were also alleviated, but to a lesser extent, by the entry of Chinese tin exports into the Western European market.

The main criticism of the International Tin Agreement in the late 1960s came from the producing countries who, after surviving the market surpluses and the quotas placed on production during the First Agreement, experienced a decade during which the market displayed a persistent tendency toward scarcity. In consequence there was a feeling in some quarters that the price of tin had been unnecessarily depressed and foreign exchange earnings limited by the Agreements. Some Malaysians even advocated their country's withdrawal from the Council's arrangements.

Experience in the early 1970s, however, would give them little support. By 1972, the market had run into surplus again and the Council responded by increasing the size of its buffer stocks. Early in the following year, however, the persistence of the surplus led the Council to impose export controls upon the producers once more in order to stabilize the situation. The strongest argument for a continuation of the International Tin Agreement is, of course, the uncertainty of the future. While the shortages of the 1960s were a fact, the prospect for the market throughout the 1970s is unclear.

On the demand side there is evidence of greater future economies in the use of tin—the can industry in the United States has begun to market a tin-free container for beverages—and the efficiency of recovering secondary tin is almost certain to increase. World demand has been characterized by an absence of significant growth in the recent past, and there is no guarantee that it will not actually fall in the future.

On the supply side, enormous uncertainty surrounds the amount of tin likely to enter the world market from the U.S.S.R. and China. And, in addition, there remains the United States' stockpile which is still in surplus and standing at nearly 255,000 tons. This figure is significantly larger than a whole year's output from the mines and smelters of the world. The known imperfections of the International Tin Agreement could easily be exceeded by the possible imperfections of a completely free market.

There has been talk of stabilizing the international lead-zinc market through an international agreement. This would be more difficult than it was for tin because there are many more producers involved, and as the number increases agreement becomes harder to achieve. A first step has been taken, however, through the International Lead and Zinc Study Group set up under the United Nations in 1959. This group meets every six months to discuss the problems of the lead-zinc industry and to make recommendations. By and large, it has served essentially as a talking-shop. However, certain of its recommendations have at times led to voluntary cutbacks by the producers in the Study Group's member countries; and, although this action has not solved the problems of the industry, the curtailment of production has, no doubt, been of some help.

The foregoing discussion has served to underline the point that there is no one answer to what a nation's mineral import policy should be in order to satisfy all the parties involved; in fact, a mineral import policy can never be wholly satisfactory to all participants. In the United States, most discussion of this problem in the past has been in Congress, where the variety of forces pulling in different directions can give a highly slanted picture. A 1962 report resulting from an RFF analysis of mineral import policy dealt with some of the factors that must be considered. The report noted that the problems themselves are difficult to formulate.

For example, a popular view of mineral import policy would have us set tariffs at levels which will maintain a "healthy" U.S. mining industry, or, as in another version, the goal is stated as a "stable and prosperous mining industry." Search as you will, there is nothing in the usual formulation of these goals that will tell us how high tariff rates should be and why. How big should each industry be? How big is healthy? Exactly what determines the extent to which demand should be satisfied from imports? And aren't health, stability, and prosperity desirable for other industries, too? Goals of this sort are too indefinite to serve as guides for policy, for the mining industries of this country can be healthy, stable, and prosperous at various levels of output and various levels of protection. (21, p. 7)

The United States has tried almost every approach to mineral imports except a total commitment to self-sufficiency. Its experience has shown that the major determining factor is the "economic exploitability" of the mineral deposit. What is "economic," of course, varies in place and in time. If, however, ore deposits are not competitive with those in other countries, it is a costly business to provide the subsidy that is required to keep them in operation. In doing so, funds are diverted that could be more effectively and profitably used in other ways, and the remaining resources of the particular mineral are further depleted. At the same time, the markets for the mineral producers of exporting countries are diminished even though these nations are often highly dependent upon the foreign exchange provided by their mineral exports. In other words, questions of mineral policy very quickly merge into the broader issues of international trade, international relations, and the development of the Third World.

6 THE LIGHT METALS:

in which it is shown how producers of these remarkably abundant mineral raw materials are striving to make a larger place for themselves in the metal market

GOLD, silver, iron, and the base metals have been known and used by man for many centuries. Other metals, even some that are quite abundant in the earth's crust, have only recently come to be used, often because they would not yield to the primitive tools and techniques of an earlier age. The light metals—aluminum, magnesium, and titanium, which make up respectively 8 percent, 2 percent, and 0.4 percent of the earth's crust—are outstandingly important among the world's newly discovered materials. They are called light metals because their relatively low specific gravity is one of their principal useful properties (figure 10); and, of the three, aluminum is in by far the greatest demand at present, although the others hold much promise for the future.

As these metals were first made available during a period of rapid technological development, many changes have been crowded into their few years of history. The light metals, products of this century, have developed in a fashion quite different from that of other metals which have century-old traditions to guide, but also to bind, them.

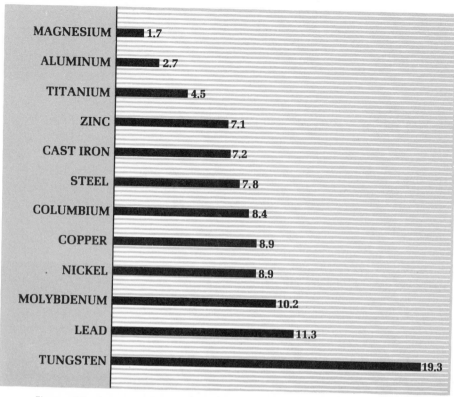

Figure 10. A comparison of the specific gravity of different metals. The weights of the light metals are seen to differ greatly from those of the base metals, the alloying metals, and steel.

ALUMINUM (an industry for which the location of suitable raw materials has proved to be less important than the availability of cheap electric power) • Aluminum is the most abundant of the metals used by man. Almost any piece of rock or lump of soil that you pick up will contain more aluminum than a rich ore contains of copper or lead or zinc. But, although aluminum is abundant, it is relatively difficult to separate from its parent rock. Consequently, from the beginning of aluminum production emphasis has been placed on finding alumina-bearing minerals that are relatively easy to reduce, and on other facets of the processing side of the industry rather than the mining side. This explains the seeming paradox that both the United States and many Western European countries import almost all of their requirements of this "abundant" material. On the other hand, there is good reason to believe that, as the most readily accessible sources of high-grade mineral material are used up, recourse will be made to relatively abundant low-grade materials. This is not a contingency facing the world in the foreseeable future, but when it occurs such materials will require an ever greater and more complex degree of processing, which will employ the further skills of the chemist and the chemical engineer (see figure 10).

A key to the present industrial development of aluminum was the discovery in 1886 of a process for the electrolytic smelting of aluminum. Scientists had been searching for such a process for many years, and when they finally were successful the identical process was discovered by two men working in two different parts of the world at approximately the same time. Charles Martin Hall, working in the United States, and Paul L. T. Héroult, in France, must share the honor for the discovery of the aluminum reduction process which bears their names.

In spite of its abundance in the earth's crust, aluminum is never found free in nature as are other metals like silver, gold, or copper. Normally it is found in combination with oxygen, and the separation of the two is very difficult. In the manufacture of aluminum, bauxite (a hydrous aluminum oxide) is first converted into an intermediate product, alumina (aluminum oxide); this in turn is reduced to aluminum metal in an electrolytic cell. Broadly speaking, 4 to 6 tons of bauxite are required to make 2 tons of alumina. These 2 tons can in turn be converted into a ton of aluminum metal, but this last step may require the use of some 15,000 kilowatt-hours of electricity. The reduction takes place in large carbon-lined pots filled with molten cryolite in which alumina is dissolved. A direct current passed through this solution causes aluminum to be deposited as a metal at the bottom of the pot which serves as the cathode, while the oxygen combines with the carbon anodes, which are lowered into the pot from above, and is released as carbon dioxide gas.

Cryolite, an unusual mineral, has played an important part in the history of aluminum development. When Charles Hall was searching for a process to make aluminum economically, he had difficulty in finding a way to melt the alumina he was using as his basic raw material. After much experimentation he discovered that alumina would dissolve in molten cryolite and that the latter would serve as an electrolyte in the reduction process. This was the fundamental discovery, and it has provided the basic process still used today in the production of aluminum. Cryolite was a key material in the discovery. This is a rare mineral to the extent that it has been found in usable quantities at only one place in the world, at Ivigtut in southwestern Greenland. However, with reserves apparently limited, a method was found to make artificial or synthetic cryolite from fluorspar, a much more common mineral. By 1969 competition from this substitute had resulted in the closure of the Ivigtut mine.

Although bauxite is but one of many potential sources of alu-

Plate 6. Dragline and bulldozer at a bauxite mine. Millions of tons of over-burden frequently have to be removed to lay bare the bauxite. (Courtesy The Aluminum Association.)

minum, it is the raw material most economic to use today. Bauxite results from the weathering of certain types of aluminum-rich rock under highly specialized climatic conditions. It occurs only in the tropics or in those areas which had a tropical climate when the bauxite was being formed. Hence, although there are some bauxite deposits in temperate climates as, for example, in Arkansas in the United States, and in southern France, Yugoslavia, and Hungary, the most important deposits of bauxite are in the tropics. Major producers of this material (table 15) are Jamaica, Australia, Surinam, the U.S.S.R., and Guyana. Their combined production represented approximately 63 percent of global output in 1970. Two years later Australia replaced Jamaica in world leadership for the production of this mineral (much of it for the Japanese market) and mined over one-fifth of the total. Very large reserves of bauxite are also known to exist in some African countries, such as Guinea and Ghana, and in parts of Asia, especially China. There is no anticipated shortage of this raw material and, in fact, many new sources are currently being brought into production.

A glance at world aluminum production figures (table 15) shows that of these ore-producing countries only the U.S.S.R. is among the major smelters of aluminum metal. Principal aluminum producers include the United States, the U.S.S.R., Canada, the E.E.C., Japan, and Norway. France, with 0.4 million tons in 1970, is the only country other than the U.S.S.R. which produces enough bauxite to supply a substantial domestic industry.

TABLE 15		Thousand tons	% of world
Major producers	(a) Bauxite:		
of bauxite and	Jamaica	12,010	21
aluminum, 1970	Australia	9,389	16
	Surinam	5,341	9
	U.S.S.R.	4,978	9
	Guyana	4,562	8
	Total	36,280	63
	World	57,988	100
	(b) Aluminum:		
	U.S.A.	3,607	37
	U.S.S.R.	1,098	11
	Canada	964	10
	E.E.C.*	950	10
	Japan	733	8
	Norway	530	5
	Total	7,992	81
	World	9,666	100

Source: U.S. Bureau of Mines (10, pp. 178 and 217).
 * Enlarged, as of 1973.

Despite the fact that major industrial countries like the United States, Britain, West Germany, and Japan are heavily deficient in bauxite, there is little concern about potential shortages of aluminum ore. There are probably three reasons for this. First, the sources from which bauxite is currently obtained—places like Jamaica, the Dominican Republic, and Haiti, in the case of the United States—have very large reserves. Second, were any of these reserves to be denied to the industrialized countries, it would not be difficult to obtain supplies from alternative sources. Third, and most important in the longer term, is the knowledge that the resources of high alumina clay or of high alumina rocks such as anorthosite are very large indeed, and that aluminum can be produced from these materials—though perhaps at a somewhat higher cost than when it is recovered from bauxite. Russia has been producing aluminum from nepheline, a rare aluminum-rich mineral, for some time. This exception is explained by a shortage of bauxite in the U.S.S.R. and a state policy of ensuring the maximum self-sufficiency possible in mineral raw materials.

At present, the use of these alternative raw materials involves the application of relatively expensive technology. For example, it has been suggested that alumina produced from anorthosite bears a cost penalty of about 12 percent per ton of aluminum ingot. However, RFF studies have shown that such cost increases can often be offset by concurrent cost reductions. In an RFF report on the major metals it is concluded that:

All this does not necessarily mean a higher cost for aluminum in the long-term future. Present cost indications are based on present technology. With allowance for the technological advances that could be expected to occur and the progress that would unquestionably be made under the economic pressures generated by the need for conversion of potential ore to ore reserves, it is reasonable to conclude that turning to lower grade aluminum resources will have minor economic repercussions, if any. Indeed, the most important cost factor is not the grade or quality of the aluminum source, but the energy required for alumina reduction. If the cost of aluminum should rise significantly, the increase would probably be due to a higher cost of electricity for aluminum processing, as the aluminum industry competes for the remaining low-cost hydropower in a world of rapidly mounting per capita energy demand. (38, p. 40)

It is clear, then, that the distribution of bauxite deposits is not the only critical factor in the longer-term pattern of the industry. Low-cost electric power has been, and prospectively will remain, a decisive factor in shaping the geography of aluminum production. It is to some examples of this geography that we now turn.

North American and West European Patterns. The U.S. aluminum industry (the world's largest) has experienced a number of shifts in the location of its major production facilities from the early days of the century. The basic pattern begins with bauxite produced from a variety of sources, mainly in the Caribbean area, and transported by ship to the Gulf Coast. Here the aluminum companies built their first cluster of alumina plants where they could be readily supplied with imported ores. The next step is the reduction process, which requires large quantities of electric power. For many years this was almost synonymous with hydroelectric power. In consequence, important concentrations of aluminum capacity were located in the Tennessee Valley, near Niagara, and especially in the Pacific Northwest. In the latter region it could take advantage of the tremendous hydroelectric power potential developed on the Columbia River and its tributaries by the Bonneville Power Administration and a series of public utility companies.

This, then, was the initial pattern of metal production for rolling mills and markets that were heavily localized in the Northeast and Middle West of the country. It is a pattern which still has its parallel in Canada, where the hydroelectric resources of Quebec and British Columbia continue to draw further aluminum investments (figure 11).

The importance of low-cost bulk supplies of electrical energy for the aluminum industry cannot be overstressed. Even when power costs are extremely low, at perhaps 2 mills per kilowatt-hour (kwh), they still can represent 8 percent of total costs, and not infrequently they make up 16 percent of a reduction plant's expenses. Naturally, therefore, aluminum producers try to locate where their power costs are low. In addition, there is the matter of bulk power availability, for an aluminum plant is a remarkably large consumer of electricity. For example, the Reynolds Metals Company, which accounts for rather more than one-fifth of the aluminum production capacity in the United States, uses more electricity each day than is required to supply the domestic needs of a metropolitan area the size of Chicago. The aluminum industry uses more electric power in one day than a town of 100,000 people might use in one year. In such circumstances the attraction of reduction plants to sites of low cost and abundant power is understandable.

But power cost is only one of a variety of expenses in aluminum production. The geographical pattern that has evolved in the aluminum industry carries with it very high transportation costs. In the production of a ton of aluminum, for instance, we might see 4 tons of bauxite mined in Jamaica and shipped perhaps 1,100 nautical miles to one of the alumina plants on the Gulf Coast to be converted into 2 tons of alumina. This material in turn might be transported some 5,000 nautical miles by sea to one of the reduction plants in the Pacific Northwest where it is converted into 1 ton of aluminum metal. Since many of the major markets are still in the northeastern part of the

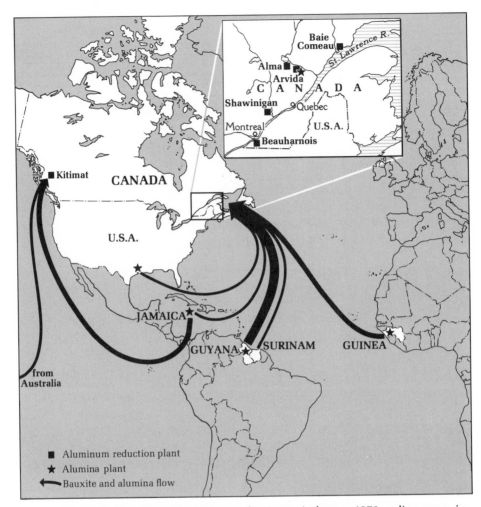

Figure 11. The Canadian primary aluminum industry, 1970, relies upon imports of bauxite and alumina, plus large domestic resources of low-cost hydropower. *Source:* Department of Energy, Mines and Resources, Canada (12).

country there is a reasonable chance that this ton of aluminum metal would be railed 2,500 miles or more across the continent to its final destination.

The magnitude of the transportation costs occasioned by this sort of movement—in sum they might total over $50 per ton of delivered ingot and represent 12–15 percent of production costs—has encouraged a steady improvement in transport technology and increasingly efficient operations. Coupled with a gradual reduction in the possibilities for producing additional low-cost hydropower, plus the fact that much of the low-cost power is already committed, these developments have encouraged the manufacturers of aluminum to locate their newest plants in entirely different areas.

The first shift away from the traditional pattern oriented toward hydroelectric power came with the building of reduction plants in the Gulf Coast area to exploit relatively low-cost power generated from natural gas or lignite fuels. The somewhat higher power costs of these plants when compared with hydroelectric power are offset by cost advantages in transportation, for the movement of alumina to distant reduction plants is eliminated. To reduce transportation costs still further, and in response to emerging regional markets, fabricating plants have in some cases been built adjacent to the Gulf Coast reduction plants. A further step away from the traditional pattern of the industry has been taken by setting up reduction capacity based on coal-generated electricity in Ohio and West Virginia. With improved coal mining technology, the fuel costs are not unreasonable—a few years ago they were as low as 4 mills per kilowatt-hour—and transportation costs are significantly reduced because these plants are located in a major market area. All the movement of the raw and reduced materials, therefore, is in the general direction of the markets. While further investments to expand capacity have continued in the traditional locations for aluminum production, these newer locations have given the industry a more complex geography and a wider range of options for future growth.

Parallel changes in locational preferences can be seen in the aluminum industry of Western Europe, where the earliest smelters in the French and Swiss Alps and in Norway, utilizing low-cost hydroelectric power, have been supplemented in recent years by newer smelters based upon the natural gas of Lacq and Groningen, and upon both coal and atomic power in Britain. However, the history of the industry in Western Europe also points to the importance of political factors and the way in which governmental assistance to aid regional development, or even the imposition of quite modest import tariffs, can offset relatively high power costs. A 9 percent tariff, for example, is approximately equivalent to power costs of some 3 mills. The economic logic of smelting aluminum in Western Europe is unquestioned. As Brubaker observed in his study of the industry, "With the present or most likely climate for trade and investment, and with the prospective relative cost positions, the primary aluminum industry is most apt to remain heavily concentrated in major industrial economies." (6, p. 10) The fact that aluminum metal cannot be transported as cheaply as the amount of alumina required to produce it is of major significance in this regard. However, the detailed geographical distribution of the industry in Western Europe—such as the location of the three British smelters, all built toward the end of the 1960s, and all located in the country's Development Areas where they are able to benefit from a variety of capital and operating cost subsidies—powerfully reflects a set of political forces operating on both the national and international scales.

Political factors also are becoming increasingly important in the location of alumina production, particularly on the international scale. In this case, the choice is frequently between investment in a developing economy and investment in a technologically advanced economy. The costs of transporting bauxite and alumina (per ton of aluminum ingot) tend to favor refining operations near the sources of the bauxite. But these can be offset by the higher labor and capital costs sometimes encountered in the developing world, due to the higher expense of building a plant there as well as the evaluation of the risks of expropriation. Frequently these cost factors cancel out and political factors finally determine location.

In recent years the leverage which can be exerted by the governments of developing countries upon the investment decisions of the large international corporations has tended to increase. Through their growing control over domestic resource exploitation and their ability to offer generous tax incentives to investment, governments in the developing world with large deposits of bauxite have been able to help attract an increasing number of alumina plants. As a consequence, production of alumina in Jamaica (1.7 million tons in 1970) and Surinam (1.0 million tons), in Guinea (0.6 million tons) and India (0.3 million tons), as well as in the more developed countries that also produce bauxite, such as Australia (2.1 million tons) and Greece (0.3 million tons), has moved steadily upwards. But their output individually lags considerably behind that of the United States and Canada, which together produced 7.7 million tons of alumina in 1970.

SUBSTITUTION AS A FACTOR IN MINERAL MARKETS • The aluminum industry is still therefore in a stage of rapid change even in the advanced industrial economies, and in many respects the whole atmosphere of the industry is quite different from that of other metals. The aluminum industry is relatively new, is aggressive, and is developing at a rapid rate; most of the other metals that have been discussed are in a more mature and rather less dynamic phase. Central to this characteristic of aluminum is its market growth.

All of the light metals are relatively new materials which do not have traditional uses and so have had to carve a place for themselves in the market for raw materials. Thus, lead was used in plumbing by the Romans, and is still used in plumbing today; but the light metals had no uses prior to this century and have had to be sold vigorously to potential users. Aluminum, which has seen spectacular growth in the past three decades, is the best example of the introduction of a

Plate 7. Ocean freighters carry bauxite from Jamaica to the United States for refining. Here, at Baton Rouge, Louisiana, crews unload the bauxite. Conveyors feed the bauxite from the dock to storage areas. (Courtesy The Aluminum Association.)

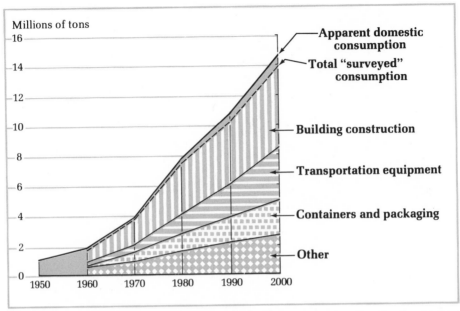

Figure 12. Trends and forecast of aluminum consumption in the United States, 1950–2000. Much greater quantities of aluminum are likely to be needed to supply the needs of a growing United States economy. This is especially evident in uses connected with construction and transportation. *Source:* Resources for the Future, unpublished estimates.

new material into the market. From 1939 to 1970 primary ingot production of aluminum in the world increased from 667,000 to 9,664,000 tons. Production in the United States during the same period increased from 148,000 to 3,606,000 tons. Even so, by 1970 aluminum consumption in the United States, where the industry is probably at its most commercially aggressive, was still only 3 percent that of steel; and the per capita consumption of aluminum was a mere 44 pounds (20 kilograms), whereas that of steel was nearly 1,300 pounds (600 kilograms). Comparisons in terms of volume rather than weight shift the emphasis slightly in the direction of the lighter metal, but the huge discrepancy remains to encourage the belief that the aluminum industry will continue its vigorous expansion for many years to come. Globally, annual growth rates of between 6 and 8 percent are regularly forecast (6, p. 54). In the RFF study, *Resources in America's Future* (25, p. 901), the middle of three forecasts showed demand in the United States increasing to 3.2 million tons in 1970, 5.7 million tons in 1980, and 14.7 million tons in the year 2000. Recognizing that actual 1970 consumption had approached 3.8 million tons, calculations made a decade later for a revised version of the same volume raised the middle projection for 1980 to 7.8 million, while retaining the year 2000 projection essentially unchanged.

The sectors of most rapid market growth for aluminum are expected to be transportation equipment, and containers and packaging, while in pure volume construction uses will continue to dominate (figure 12). In some of these markets aluminum is going into quite new uses for which its own characteristics are particularly advantageous—for example, certain types of pleasure boats and house trailers. In other markets, aluminum is being utilized in long-established products and replaces another material, often another metal such as steel or copper.

The fact that mineral materials can and do replace one another is important when we consider long-term mineral supply, for it emphasizes the point that many uses of materials are quite flexible. Thus, Americans have traditionally used wood siding for their homes, but in recent years aluminum siding has moved into this market because technical developments can make aluminum an attractive substitute for wood. In the future some new method of treating wood may reverse this trend, or some new plastic may present yet another alternative. No one product is essential in all its uses. There is a high degree of interchangeability among raw materials, based on a complex relationship between price, quality, availability, and a number of other factors which include price stability and service. During wartime, when price becomes a relatively less important factor and many sources of supply are cut off, one catches a glimpse of the real scope of substitutability; one extreme example was the use of silver as a substitute for copper during World War II. Silver is a better conductor of electricity, but normally is not widely used because of its price.

Aluminum, then, in its march to higher levels of production and use, has been substituted for other metals because it can perform some functions better at the same cost or as well at a lower one. It has replaced steel in bus and railroad coach bodies, lead in certain types of cable covering, copper in electrical transmission lines, and tin as well as steel in containers. At the same time, other nonmetallic materials—plastics, glass, ceramics, wood products—are being substituted for metals and for one another. Metals move back into markets previously held by one or another of these alternative materials. There is, in fact, a continuing interchange of raw materials.

This interchange has been accelerated by advances in technology, the frequent birth of new materials, the development of new alloys, and such changing demands of the market as the trend towards a preference for lighter materials. Because of this, most markets have a choice in the materials that they will use. Some branches of the mineral industry with long traditions for supplying particular markets have been somewhat slow to recognize this fact. They have been slow to respond to competition and have failed to invest in product research. Today, and increasingly in the future, the demand is not for steel or aluminum or copper, but rather is for a material capable of performing a certain task effectively and economically. This material may be steel or aluminum or copper; it may be plastic or glass or fiber. The choice in the market economies will be a business decision based on a blend of competitive economics combined with some elements of tradition.

The relative position of aluminum among the metals has been improving steadily over the years. Figure 13, based on unpublished projections in progress for an updated version of *Resources in America's Future* (25), shows how the demand for metals is expected to shift in one advanced economy during the remainder of this century with aluminum increasing its share from around 10 percent in 1960 to 18 percent in 2000. Some observations should be made about this chart. First, it is merely a forecast projected under specified assumptions, and it is unlikely that all of these will come true. The chart nevertheless gives a good idea of the most likely direction of change. Second, this consumption estimate is based on volume rather than tonnage—not the usual approach but one believed to afford a better basis for comparison. Thus, aluminum, because of its lightness, shows up relatively well. This lightness is one of aluminum's advantages and

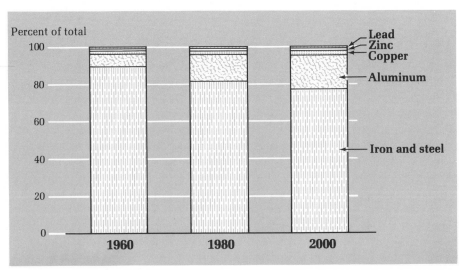

Figure 13. Past and estimated future consumption of metals in the United States, 1960, 1980, and 2000. Recent consumption patterns, shown here on a volume basis, indicate that over the next thirty years aluminum will encroach upon many of the uses now performed by steel. *Source:* Resources for the Future, unpublished estimates.

should be underscored in any comparison. Third, percentages like these can easily be misread. Here, for example, they indicate that steel will drop in its share from some 86 percent of the metal used in the United States to around 77 percent. Some might interpret this as evidence that the use of steel will decrease. However, with growing populations and rising standards of living during the rest of the century, the use of all metals will increase; and in terms of quantity, on both a tonnage basis and a volume basis, steel consumption is almost certain to increase more than aluminum.

MAGNESIUM (in the case of this metal, the usable raw materials are essentially unlimited) • Magnesium has followed much the same path as aluminum, but has never quite reached the "take-off" point at which consumption begins to expand rapidly. Annual production for 1970 in the United States, the U.S.S.R., and Norway contributed 84 percent to the world total output of 214,000 tons (table 16). This is a much more modest figure than world aluminum output, which in the same year was forty-five times larger.

The more widespread use of aluminum derives from the fact that the two metals share many characteristics and are competitive in many of the same markets. But while magnesium is about one-third lighter than aluminum, it is also about 25 percent more expensive. The aluminum industry became established at an earlier date than the magnesium industry and was able to produce plentiful material at a relatively low cost. Hence, aluminum gained a foothold in the markets that it serves, and because there is relatively little utility or cost advantage between it and magnesium it has been able to maintain and, through continuing research, even expand upon its early advantage.

Magnesium enjoys what must be the strongest raw material position of any metallic mineral, for it is recovered from sea water. About a cubic mile (4 cubic kilometers) of sea water contains some 6.4 mil-

TABLE 16		_Thousand tons_	_% of world_
Major producers of	U.S.A.	102	47
primary magnesium,	U.S.S.R.	45	21
1970	Norway	35	16
	E.E.C.*	14	7
	Japan	10	5
	Canada	8	4
	Total	214	100
	World	214	100

Source: U.S. Bureau of Mines (10, p. 680).
   * Enlarged, as of 1973.

lion tons of magnesium—not so high a figure when one considers that magnesium represents only 0.13 percent of the content of sea water and that the same volume of sea water would weigh almost 4,750 million tons. It is possible to extract magnesium from sea water economically, and this is the major source for the United States which accounted for about 47 percent of world output in 1970. However, since magnesium can be, and is, produced from other sources, such as the minerals dolomite and magnesite, there is no foreseeable shortage of the raw materials from which magnesium is produced.

The history of magnesium manufacture throughout the world has been powerfully molded by political forces. The metal was first produced commercially in Germany in 1886, and until the outbreak of World War I most of the world's supplies came from that country. U.S. production began in 1915. Several companies entered the field at about this time, but by 1920 these had narrowed down to the Dow Chemical Company and a subsidiary of the Aluminum Company of America, which dropped out in 1927. By this time, however, German producers were reasserting their commercial supremacy in this field. They had developed a worldwide market for their output by 1930 and as a result American output of magnesium had shrunk to about 3,000 tons by the end of the decade.

Then came World War II. As with aluminum, wartime demands for aircraft production and other military uses led to a phenomenal increase in American output. Production rose from 5,700 tons in 1940 to 44,400 in 1942, and then to a peak of 166,500 tons in 1943. However, American output was back to 4,800 tons three years later and since then it has continued to fluctuate widely. With the Korean and Vietnam wars, the country's needs increased substantially, while in the intervening years demand fell away abruptly. West Germany, in the meantime, became the principal destination of American magnesium exports.

Private companies could not possibly handle fluctuations in demand of this magnitude. For many years, in fact, the bulk of American production was in government plants. Thus, in 1943, fifteen plants were in operation, of which thirteen were owned by the government. By July of 1944, five of the government plants had closed, four others were on limited operations, and by November of 1945 only one plant—that of Dow Chemical at Freeport, Texas—was in production. For many years Dow, with a plant at Velasco, Texas, as well as Freeport, and with the blessing of successive administrations, dominated the American market. It still has by far the largest production capacity in the United States (109,000 tons per year in 1970). However, while government plants were reactivated to serve the upsurge of military needs during the Korean War, production increases during the middle and late 1960s have been associated with an expanding role for the

American Magnesium Company in Snyder, Texas (27,000 tons). The 1970s will see the further erosion of the Dow monopoly as new facilities in Utah (based upon the brines of the Great Salt Lake) and in Washington State (using local dolomite) are completed.

The parallels between the structure of the aluminum and magnesium industries in the United States are worth recalling at this point. Both industries followed a somewhat similar pattern before World War II. Although production of aluminum was much higher than that of magnesium, there was only one producer for each metal—Alcoa for aluminum, Dow for magnesium. Their wartime experience was also similar: a great expansion of capacity was financed largely by the government. At the war's end, however, the story changed. The government more or less forced competition upon aluminum by refusing to sell any government plants to Alcoa and by disposing of several of them to new and somewhat reluctant producers (Kaiser and Reynolds) under terms they could not afford to reject. Subsequently other producers, such as Alusuisse and Péchiney, also entered the market.

In the case of magnesium, however, there were no new producers; most of the plants were closed down, and in 1957 Dow was allowed to buy one of the big government plants, thereby more than doubling its capacity and maintaining its position as the sole producer. The industry continued to be characterized by all the features of monopoly. There was one major producer, Dow; it had significant excess capacity, thereby discouraging the entry of new firms into the market; and prices were not related to demand. The price of magnesium rose steadily from 54 cents per kilogram in 1952 to 78 cents in 1956; since then it has remained constant in dollar terms, while production has fluctuated from less than 30,000 tons to over 120,000 tons.

Before World War II, the growth of the market for aluminum in the United States was in some measure constrained by the fact that there was only one producer. Manufacturers did not want to design a material into their products if it could be obtained from only one source. Certainly, the belief that competition stimulates the development of new markets, and also leads to research into new uses and forms of a material, has been confirmed by the postwar history of the aluminum industry. Not only has the industry recovered from the fall-off in demand in the early years of peace, but it has gone on to set a series of new production records. It has been suggested that the former monopolistic position of Dow Chemical in the case of magnesium played some part in the failure of that metal to exhibit a similar vigor in its market growth. However, now that the monopoly is being challenged, these notions will be put to the test. There are many who believe that the 1970s will see the emergence of many more non-military uses for the metal and that the magnesium industry will move into a phase of more sustained growth.

TITANIUM (which in its early days was called the miracle metal) • Titanium occupies a somewhat uncertain place among the metals. It is abundant—there is more titanium in the earth's crust than there is copper, lead, zinc, tin, and nickel put together. Its principal ores, ilmenite and rutile, are mined in many parts of the world, but especially in Canada, Australia, the United States, and Norway (table 17). Its physical characteristics provide the metal with many opportunities for widespread use, since its strength-to-weight ratio is higher than that of any commonly used metal and it is unusually resistant to corrosion.

Titanium has often been hailed as the "metal of the future," but its current use as a metal is still relatively small (see table 17). Its potential utility in many forms—as an oxide, alloy, or metal—is surpassed by few other materials, but as yet it does not satisfy really large-scale demands. Like magnesium, it still needs to establish a central place in the market for metals. Like all the light metals, it is difficult to separate from its ores. However—and this is an important difference—unlike aluminum, the necessary technology that will lead to really low-cost titanium production has yet to be discovered. Thus, in 1970 aluminum metal sold for approximately $640 per ton in the U.S. market where 3.6 million tons were produced; in the same year titanium sponge, still only an intermediate form of the metal, sold for about $3,000 per ton (down from $11,000 two decades earlier), while American output was less than 15,000 tons.

Titanium is used in a number of forms. In the United States the main use, accounting for over 90 percent of demand, is not as a metal but as an oxide in the manufacture of paint. Its remarkable covering powers and resistance to weather produce a brilliant lasting white

TABLE 17			*Thousand tons*	*% of world*
Major producers	(a) Ilmenite:			
of titanium		Canada	2,258	44
concentrates,		Australia	879	17
1970		U.S.A.	787	15
		Norway	579	11
		Finland	151	3
		Total	4,654	90
		World*	5,100	100
	(b) Rutile:			
		Australia	368	88
		Sierra Leone	44	11
		Total	412	99
		World*	417	100

Source: Institute of Geological Sciences (22, p. 363).
* Excluding U.S.S.R.

paint. As an alloying metal, it is added to steel in the ladle, where it acts as a deoxidizer and cleanser. Ingot production of titanium in the United States grew from nothing prior to 1946 to a peak of 26,000 tons in 1969. Titanium sponge, the intermediate product in metal production, is produced for both domestic and export markets also in Japan, Britain, and the U.S.S.R.

Titanium metal, which is our particular concern here, was developed for use in military aircraft. In the early 1950s, when military thinking was in terms of faster and higher-flying manned aircraft, titanium with its unique properties was seen as the answer to many problems. At the time, it was being produced in quantities of only a few hundred tons a year, but the United States government, in an effort to get enough metal for anticipated needs, actively supported the development of new capacity. Then came a series of setbacks for titanium. Steelmakers were able to improve the quality of their alloys so that they could meet at lower costs some of the new metal requirements of the aircraft industry. The cost cuts which were supposed to bring titanium prices down to a more reasonable range were impressive, but still they could not overcome the competitive pressure of steel and other materials. Above all, demand fell abruptly as, with the shift to guided missiles, production of military aircraft was cut back. For a time, at least, the bottom dropped out of the market for titanium metal; new specifications favored other materials; and the vast fleets of bombers and fighters carrying titanium engines and structures never materialized. Today the major uses of the metal are still in aircraft— the 1970 market in the United States was split 53 percent for jet engines, 25 percent for airframes, 9 percent for space and missiles, and 13 percent for other industrial uses—but total consumption was very much lower than had at one time been expected.

Titanium today might well be classed as one of the minor metals —a rather broad group of materials used in fairly small quantities for special purposes, often in connection with aerospace technology, atomic power, and research at high temperatures and pressures. This group would include a host of uncommon names: beryllium, zirconium, cesium, selenium, rubidium. Such materials are relatively expensive because they are produced and used in quite small quantities. Titanium may be able to break out of this association in time, for it has a large potential market if its price can be reduced to a point where it is more competitive—and its price has been dropping quite rapidly over the twenty-five year period that the metal has been in use. However, that time has not yet arrived, and it still remains appropriate to regard titanium as essentially "the metal of the future."

7 INDUSTRIAL MINERALS AND ROCKS: in which group there are associated a vast array of nonmetallic minerals ranging from diamonds to sand

METALLIC mineral deposits, in occurrences of sufficient concentration to be of interest to the miner, underlie only a small part of the earth's surface. Even the largest copper or iron deposits extend over only a few square kilometers. Most of the surface of the globe is underlain by rock of many different varieties made up of hundreds of different minerals, most of which either are of no great economic value to society or occur in concentrations unusable at this time.

Some of the common rocks are of more than ordinary use, however. Indeed, in terms of value, they are among man's most important mineral materials. For example, in 1970 the value of sand and gravel produced in the United States was slightly more than the value of iron ore, more than half the value of the copper content of copper ore, and about 80 percent more than the value of uranium ore. The value of phosphate rock was greater than the value of molybdenum, lead, and zinc individually—and copper, iron, molybdenum, lead, zinc, and uranium, in that order, were the top value metals produced in the country. (The figures upon which these comparisons are based are from the *Minerals Yearbook* [10, pp. 106, 107]; although they may not always be strictly comparable, they do give a reasonably accurate idea of the relative value of these varied mineral commodities.) The industrial rocks exhibit such physical and chemical diversity and have such a wide range of uses that it is difficult to make valid generalizations about them. But with some exceptions (phosphate rock is one) they are relatively common and have value because they occur near to places where they can be readily used.

Industrial minerals, on the other hand, are much less common, but are still produced in significant quantities. The value of salt produced in the United States in 1970, for example, was greater than that of any metallic mineral except copper and iron ore; and the value of gypsum production was more than half the value of gold production. In recent years the total value of production of these industrial minerals and rocks together has been nearly one and one-half times that of metallic minerals—although the gap between the two has been tending to narrow.

The constituents of this rather ill-defined group have one thing in common: they are not metallic, and they are often called nonmetallic minerals rather than industrial minerals and rocks. The terms are used interchangeably, but it should be remembered that "nonmetallic minerals" covers the whole field, while the term "industrial minerals and rocks" can be split to consider only the industrial minerals or only the industrial rocks. Included in the nonmetallics, then, can be any mineral material not classified as a metal or as a mineral fuel. In some classifications even the mineral fuels are considered as nonmetallics which, of course, they are. It is because of this vagueness that the term "industrial minerals and rocks" is of value even though it may sound unnecessarily awkward. It usefully divides a vast array of materials into those that are rocks (such as granite or limestone) and products of the decomposition of rocks (such as sand or clay), and those that are minerals (such as salt or gypsum or asbestos). Within these two classes a further distinction is made according to the industrial use made of the various materials.

Some of the industrial minerals (such as gypsum) have much in common with the metals and are mined, processed, and marketed according to much the same patterns. On the other hand, some of the largest components of the nonmetallic mineral industry are in many ways quite different from the metal industry, and indeed, some producing companies (e.g., producers of sand and gravel) are somewhat mystified when they find themselves included in a survey of the mineral industry. Nevertheless, it is customary to classify them as a part of this industry, and statistics on such materials as clay, gravel, gypsum, and mica are to be found in the *Minerals Yearbook* of the U.S. Bureau of Mines, alongside copper, lead, zinc, and the other metals.

How do these materials differ from metallic minerals? One important factor relates to the unit value of the material involved. Metals such as copper, zinc, or nickel are priced in terms of cents per kilogram or even, in the case of gold and platinum, in terms of dollars per gram. Nonmetallic minerals, on the other hand, are usually priced in terms of dollars per ton—in some cases $5 to $25 per ton, as with salt or sulfur, and in some cases little more than $1 per ton, as with some types of sand and limestone. The diamond, a nonmetallic mineral, would hardly fall into this class; but, as has been seen, almost every generalization about the mineral industry has its exceptions.

Quantity is another factor of differentiation. Nonmetallic minerals are used in very large quantities. In most cases they are mined or quarried quite close to the place where they are used, simply because transport over any significant distance would raise their costs substantially. Sand and gravel or crushed rock, for example, are rarely transported more than a few miles. Long-distance shipping within a country is relatively limited with all nonmetallics, and international trade is quite unusual. On these counts alone, the general characteristics of the industry are somewhat different from those of the metallic minerals. It follows that although we find many of the same problems, constraints, and characteristics that are associated with the metallic minerals, there is a shift in emphasis as to which features are important and which are less important. This springs fundamentally from the fact that we are dealing with bulky materials of low value. The value per unit of weight (or price per ton) of industrial rocks is particularly low, since rock materials suitable for most needs are quite widespread and they can be mined and processed cheaply. Sometimes they require no processing at all.

Although local conditions exert a much stronger influence on the total picture than they do in the case of the metals industry, there are important exceptions among the industrial minerals. Mica, and asbestos and graphite—all of which are somewhat uncommon—fall into this group. These materials are used for special purposes in much the same form as that in which they are found in nature; and since nature has put together the earth's crust with almost infinite variety, the physical characteristics of the material taken from particular deposits can have considerable importance. Graphite from Madagascar is not the same as graphite from Ceylon, whereas lead from Peru is interchangeable with lead from Missouri or Australia. The two graphite materials are not completely interchangeable in a particular market and do not have the same value. Similarly, the value of mica depends on the size and purity of the crystals, which vary greatly from one deposit to another. Diamonds, graphite, mica, asbestos, garnet, and some other industrial minerals which are marketed in their natural state come in many different grades. These grades depend on their physical characteristics, which are often associated with individual deposits of the mineral, and thus some industrial minerals do enter world trade.

Even with materials valued at no more than one or two dollars a ton, however, physical characteristics are important. Limestone, for example, is used extensively as an aggregate in making concrete, but all limestone is not acceptable for this use. Some beds of limestone are too porous or contain zones of weakness and cannot meet the specifications for the particular project under consideration. In this situation, other sources of suitable aggregate must be found, and are usually available, nearby. While there are a number of other characteristics setting the nonmetallics apart from the metallic minerals, their low unit value and the importance of their natural physical form are the most significant.

Of the nonmetallic minerals in the United States, over 70 percent by value are construction materials of the most common sort—sand and gravel, stone, clay, and cement (which is made from limestone and clay). These raw materials are widespread, cheap, and are extracted from a large number of local sources throughout the world. They show quite a different facet of the mineral industry, a facet to which attention should be paid because of the magnitude of this side of the industry. In many instances industrial mineral producers have already faced the problems of bulk handling and sorting of materials and of adjusting to zoning regulations in areas of high populations. Both of these factors will undoubtedly become more important to other branches of the mineral industry in time.

The division between industrial rocks and industrial minerals is far from rigid, but as a generalization the industrial minerals lie somewhere between rocks and metallic minerals. Thus, they are low in value, but are generally worth several times as much as rock. (A ton of limestone is worth about $1.50; of sulfur, about $25.00; and of lead, some $350.) Transportation costs may restrict their market area, but they nevertheless do enter international trade. Indeed, sulfur has some characteristics resembling those of metals more than those of industrial rocks, and may serve as a bridge between the two.

SULFUR (in which technology has made available an unexpected variety of sources in recent years) • Sulfur is one of the nonmetallic materials which is classed as an industrial mineral rather than as a rock. In industry it has considerable importance, for this brimstone of the ancients and spring tonic of more recent days has become a key raw material for one of the fastest growing and most important segments of a modern economy, the chemical industry.

The value of U.S. sulfur production in 1970, amounting to 39 percent of world elemental output, was over $150 million, a figure exceeded among the metallic minerals only by copper, iron ore, molybdenum, lead, and zinc; yet one hears relatively little of sulfur for most of it goes into the early stages of manufacturing. Some 87 percent of world production is converted into sulfuric acid (a ton of elemental sulfur will produce about 3 tons of 100 percent sulfuric acid) and approximately 50 percent of all sulfur produced in the United States is used in the manufacture of fertilizer. Other branches of the chemical industry consume an additional 30 percent, and petroleum refining, iron and steel production, and other branches of mineral processing also require significant amounts. These various markets have increased the demand for sulfur substantially over the last twenty-five years, although something of a demand plateau appears to have been reached in the late 1960s.

A number of the characteristics of the mineral industries that are common to the metallic minerals and nonmetals alike—fixed location, depletion of reserves, changing patterns of supply, competition between primary and by-product production, the place of technology —are excellently illustrated by the history of sulfur. (See ref. 19.)

At the close of the last century some 95 percent of the world's elemental sulfur came from the mines of Sicily. High price and limited production from this natural monopoly restricted the use of sulfur but stimulated the search for new sources. The first such source put to general use was pyrite, an iron sulfide which is quite common throughout the world and which today still accounts for a small part of world sulfur production. Its initial development took place over a hundred years ago and served to lessen the hold of the Italian sulfur producers for some uses, but they still remained the major suppliers of the pure element.

The great advance came after 1891, when Herman Frasch patented a process for recovering the sulfur which forms a cap over some of the salt domes or plugs deep beneath the Gulf Coast of Texas, Louisiana, and Mexico. The process was so successful that it completely changed the pattern of the sulfur industry. Italian control was broken for all time and the economy of Sicily suffered a serious blow. Although the Frasch process may have been an unfortunate invention for Sicily, it was a technological stroke of luck for the world, for Sicilian production could have supplied only a fraction of the sulfur man has since consumed. The deposits of Sicily were not exhausted. Indeed, they still produce small quantities of sulfur, as they have for several hundred years; in this they serve to illustrate the fact that the death of a mineral deposit is rarely a sudden and drastic end but rather a slow tapering off which can continue almost indefinitely. In this case a traditional source of a mineral raw material was replaced by a completely new source, made available by a significant breakthrough in technology. Sulfur from this new source was cheaper, vastly more abundant, and capable of meeting the growing demands of a rapidly industrializing world at just the time when the need was becoming acute.

The Gulf Coast sulfur-bearing salt domes are remarkable geologic structures which so far appear to be unique in the world. They form an almost limitless reserve of salt; they have yielded vast quantities of oil; and during this century they have also supplied the bulk of the world's sulfur. Sulfur melts at about 240° Fahrenheit (115° Celsius). The Frasch process takes advantage of this through pumping water heated above this temperature into the sulfur-bearing formation. The sulfur melts away from the adjacent rock and impurities, and is pumped to the surface, where it solidifies in an almost chemically pure form.

There are over 200 salt domes in the Gulf Coast area of Texas, Louisiana, and Mexico but only a few of these are sulfur-bearing. First one, then two, and now eight producing companies are using the Frasch process to recover sulfur from the handful of domes that have yielded to commercial exploitation. It was upon these few locations in this limited area that the United States—and, in fact, the world—depended for so long for a major part of their supply of elemental sulfur. However, as with all mineral deposits, the supply is not unlimited. Although the domes are an abundant source of sulfur, and will continue to contribute to world supply for a long time, it was clear as early as the 1950s that their reserves would not indefinitely be capable of meeting both national and international demands. By that time some of the domes had been exhausted and had been closed down. Although new mines continued to be opened through the 1960s (including some offshore developments, up to 8 miles [12 kilometers] from land and in 50 feet [15 meters] of water), it became increasingly clear that the most productive period of the sulfur domes was drawing to a close. While producers in Texas and Louisiana were in a position to maintain and even increase output if required, additional sources were demonstrably required if the supply of sulfur on world markets was to keep pace with growing demand.

The first response of the industry was to develop the adjacent resources in Mexico where the Frasch process could be used to exploit deposits similar (but in certain respects inferior) to those of the United States Gulf Coast. By 1970 Mexico was the sixth largest producer of elemental sulfur in the world, mining 6 percent of global output (table 18). More important in the long run, however, was the discovery that sulfur could be removed from acid gas streams, as a result of which natural and refinery gases have become a major new reserve of the mineral. Sulfur removed from natural gas in Canada especially, but also in France, the United States, and (prospectively) in the Middle East, quickly transformed an emerging world shortage into a world glut. For over a decade now prices, with some fluctuations, have gradually softened, and some of the higher-cost Frasch mines have been forced out of production. Thus, the recent history

TABLE 18

		Thousand tons	% of world
Major producers of	U.S.A.	8,667	39
elemental sulfur,	Canada	4,442	20
1970	Poland	2,710	12
	France	1,733	8
	U.S.S.R.	1,599	7
	Mexico	1,380	7
	Total	20,531	93
	World	22,096	100

Source: U.S. Bureau of Mines (10, p. 1068).

of the sulfur industry illustrates how the world was threatened by a mineral shortage; yet how, once again, the stimulus provided by this potential shortage, combined with technology, has ensured the availability of a new and important source at the right moment. This rather dramatic act has been played out many times during the history of mineral development.

BY-PRODUCTS AND POLLUTION CONTROL • Sulfur output from "sour gas" is a by-product material and is therefore endowed with certain important characteristics. The production of natural gas from the fields of Alberta and British Columbia in Canada (which provide large and increasing quantities of fuel for the growing markets of the west coast of North America), from the Lacq field of southwestern France, and from a host of smaller fields such as those of Wyoming in the United States automatically brings with it the by-production of sulfur. In producing this natural gas, the sulfur cannot be ignored since it must be removed as an objectionable constituent. Thus, sulfur from this source will be made available whether there is a market for it or not. And since its cost of production is low, it can be sold for whatever price it will bring in the market, with potentially disrupting effects upon the traditional producers of sulfur. To date, the sulfur has been sold and in some cases it provides as much as 50 percent of the total return on production. Naturally, this is a source of considerable satisfaction to the gas companies, for it is a bonus which does much more than cover the inevitable costs of separation.

By-production also means that the market for natural gas has begun to exert a high degree of control over the supply of sulfur and that further supplies of sulfur will be made available in response to that market rather than the demand for sulfur. In the present and prospective state of energy markets, there is ample evidence that the supply of sulfur from natural "sour gas" sources will continue to increase. In addition, the growing importance placed upon the reduction of air pollution in the industrially advanced nations, and in particular the reduction of sulfur dioxide emissions from refineries, power stations, iron and steel works, and the like, has begun to provide yet a further new source of sulfur and sulfuric acid supplies.

For perspective, total world production of sulfur in all forms in 1970 was 32.5 million tons of sulfur equivalent: of this, just over 10 million was from Frasch process operations in the United States, Mexico, and Poland; about 3 million was from sulfur ores (especially in the United States and Poland); about 9 million was recovered as a by-product from the purification of natural and refinery gas; and 10.4 million was contained in pyrites. The pyrites—mainly produced in the U.S.S.R., Japan, and Spain—are sulfide ores from which sulfuric acid is produced directly without going through an elemental sulfur stage. Thus we talk of sulfur equivalent. Of the three principal sources, it has been the output of by-product sulfur from natural gas that has grown the fastest in recent years.

Environmental concerns and, in particular, the growing controls over air-polluting activities have been aimed increasingly at sulfur dioxide emissions, since their harmful effects are widely recognized. In consequence, the prospects now are that with the increasing removal of sulfur from natural gas and petroleum, from coal and non-ferrous minerals, a superabundance of sulfur will be made available to the world economy. It has been suggested that if all the sulfur is recovered from those sulfur-bearing minerals that are destined for other uses, by the year 2000 supply will exceed demand by a factor of two or more. Thus the traditional industry based upon the Frasch process is now seriously threatened in the medium term, and the most urgent need of the industry is to find large new uses for sulfur that can help to bring about a better balance between future demand and supply.

The impact of environmental controls upon the sulfur dioxide emissions of the mineral industries is potentially much more far-reaching than just their effect on the sulfur market. Because most copper, lead, and zinc ores are sulfides, their associated smelting operations generate considerable quantities of sulfur fumes and par-ticulates, which have been traditionally released into the atmosphere on a large scale. In recent years, however, new federal and state regulations in the United States have been introduced to limit these emissions severely. This in turn has led to a shutdown of some domestic zinc smelters and to the reduced or intermittent operation of others. Reductions in smelter capacity have in turn caused mine production of nonferrous metals and their by-products to be cut back.

The copper industry in the United States, along with (high-sulfur) coal mining, is in a particularly sensitive position. The Environmental Protection Agency is insisting that the industry take measures during the 1970s to reduce noxious emissions from its smelters.

Whether it can bear these costs and remain at its present scale, or whether marginal operations will decide to withdraw from production, remains an open question. How these cost increases will affect the competitive position of U.S. producers in the world market is also uncertain.

Anti-pollution legislation has still further implications for the mining industry. The industry's mineral reserve position is defined in part on the basis of mining and smelting costs. In the short run, insofar as some of the technology required to reduce pollution is untested, an additional element of risk is added to the industry's problems. Additional risks mean additional costs over and above the known costs of pollution control. It is very possible that some revisions will have to be made to the reserve position of some mineral deposits and mining localities because of increased costs arising from emerging environmental priorities. Thus, while sulfur is likely to become more abundant, perhaps too abundant, as a consequence of pollution control legislation, copper supplies could well become somewhat more difficult to maintain at present levels and the geography of their availability may have to be partly revised.

LIMESTONE (in which some of the problems of mineral development in heavily populated areas and the increasing importance of environmental quality are noted) • Limestone is one of the most common, abundant, and widespread rock types in the crust of the earth. It is a sedimentary rock made up of calcium carbonate which was laid down in the sea bed during past geologic ages when shallow seas covered large parts of today's continents. Limestone formations underlie some 15 to 20 percent of the United States and outcrop extensively in hills and mountains. It is probably the most useful and widely used common rock type in the earth.

The quantity of limestone used in a modern economy places limestone mining or quarrying among the largest mining industries in many countries. However, since the recovery of limestone is carried on at hundreds of relatively small operations rather than concentrated in a few locations, the industry is not normally regarded as being particularly large or important. In 1970, nearly 530 million tons of limestone were produced in the United States. The greater part of this material (over 60 percent) was used as an aggregate in concrete and road construction. Other major uses are in the making of cement, as a flux in metallurgical processes, as an agricultural soil conditioner, and in the manufacture of lime. In each of these uses it is the chemical characteristics of the limestone that make it valuable.

In the cement industry, limestone and a source of silica, often clay, are mixed in proper proportions and are heated as they tumble through the length of a slowly revolving inclined kiln. The raw materials enter at the upper end of the kiln, a blast of intense flame jets into the kiln from the other end, and by the time the raw materials have worked their way down the slope to the heated end of the kiln they have been converted into a cement material. The clinkers of cement are ground to a powder, mixed with gypsum which controls the setting time of the final product, and are marketed in bulk or in bags. The major markets are in the largest centers of population, so there are advantages in locating cement plants as close as possible to large urban and industrial complexes, or at least locating them where they have low-cost transportation to those complexes. Such a proximity of cement manufacture and urban development is not without its problems, for the control of flue dust and noxious emissions is a costly business.

Lime is manufactured in kilns similar to but smaller than those used in the cement industry. The objective here is less complex: it is to remove the carbon dioxide from the calcium carbonate of limestone, leaving as the final product lime, a calcium oxide important to the chemical industry. Lime is this industry's principal low-cost alkali raw material; it is the basic equivalent of sulfur.

The largest market for limestone is, however, aggregates. Aggregate in this sense means any hard, inert substance that can be mixed with a cementing material to form a concrete. The value of an aggregate depends on not only its physical characteristics but its location, for this is a material used in very large quantities and it must be cheap. Limestone often fits these requirements, but any suitable material can be used if it is found close to the area of demand. Sand and gravel, for example, are highly acceptable because they have good physical characteristics and are easy to recover. Indeed, the combined production of sand and gravel in the United States exceeds that of any metallic mineral and amounted to over 850 million tons in 1970. Granite or basalt or slag are also used as an aggregate in some areas.

THE MINERAL INDUSTRY AND LAND USE CONFLICTS • The major market for aggregates is in construction and road building, and the majority of construction and road-building projects are in areas of concentrated population. Here is a situation in which the mineral industry, normally located far from centers of heavy population, is operating in densely settled areas. Here is at least one case where the public does have some close contact with mineral development. In consequence, it is possible to examine the interrelationship of the two, and perhaps to see something of the problems that other branches of the mining industry are likely to face as populations and incomes increase and as larger tracts of country become more heavily settled and travelled. With growing demand for recreation, and particularly recreation in relatively unspoilt natural surroundings, even remote mining areas are no longer as isolated as they once were. Mining companies can expect increasing public interest in their activities and greater surveillance over their behavior.

In one form or another, conflicts over the use of land for mining have arisen since early days of the industry. To see the destruction of familiar or beautiful scenery is as offensive as to experience the steady deterioration of streams, lakes, estuaries, and atmosphere. These destructive side effects are, to some extent, inherent in the mining industry. They can be limited or repaired, but only at a cost. The producers of aggregate are engaged in a business that often must be noisy, dusty, and destructive of landscape. But it is a highly competitive business which requires them to locate operations as close as possible to their major markets. With their raw material valued in 1970 at less than $3.00 per ton, and in some areas as little as $1.55, high transport costs can easily erode away their profit. As a consequence, the industry's pits and quarries often are in close physical contact with the outward surge of suburban development which, in fact, may require these reserves of aggregate material for its own construction.

A principal factor inhibiting the market orientation of the industry is the high cost of land close to areas of dense population; this to some extent offsets the economies of transportation. A second restraint is the number and stringency of zoning regulations and laws in areas near centers of heavy population. People may well have moved to the suburbs to escape the noise and discomforts of city life; they naturally will oppose pits and quarries in their midst—the noise and dust, the great holes left in the ground after the recoverable material has been removed, the possibilities of danger for children. These sentiments become institutionalized in land use planning regulations.

However, because city building costs would rise if nearby aggregate materials were not used, some form of compromise has to be reached. Sometimes operations are restricted to daylight hours. Sometimes shrubs and hedges are planted along the sides of pits and between the operations and the highways. Worked-out pits can be restored, in some cases by refilling and using them for housing developments, in others by grading and transforming the areas into parks and recreation areas containing artificial lakes. Steep-walled rock quarries pose more difficult problems, though even here some reclamation is possible. However, some rock quarries have already begun to reduce potential conflicts by shifting from open pit to underground mining, and have even found that there is a market near urban areas for the fireproof mined-out space.

Attitudes toward the aggregate industry, and indeed toward all quarrying and mining activities, may well change as experience is gained in modern methods of mineral exploitation and improved after-treatment of land. Conservation awards to some mining companies in the United States have drawn attention to the possibilities of good industrial practice. Mineral extraction is by no means a permanent form of land use, but there is no denying that, however well planned, mining operations must result in a temporary and sometimes a permanent change—even if it is not a deterioration—in the local environment.

It is clear that different degrees of environmental change are possible with all mining activities. Each can be associated with a different level of costs. In the case of the aggregate industry, given the high cost of product transport and the local nature of the activity, it is fortunate that higher environmental standards and the related higher costs must be reconciled within the same community. The opportunities for reasoned choice between different environmental benefits and their contrasting levels of expense can be decided locally; the issues are cleanly drawn. But in the case of the metallic mineral industries the problems are more complex. Curtailment of mining activities in an area of outstanding natural beauty may be sought with special zeal, let us say, by a distant urban community many of whose inhabitants are keen conservationists. Yet it could well be that most of the social costs of such a policy would be borne by a more local community—probably an isolated mining and smelting town whose people could face economic disaster if their activities were to be curtailed. While in the long view there is an irrefutable case for the mining industry to respect environmental priorities, in the short term a society has conflicting goals among which must be ranked some stability of mining employments. Typically, with modern environmental and land use decisions, the gainers and the losers are different people, and in this situation new institutions are required through which the conflicts can be equitably resolved.

Land use conflicts on a national scale pose further problems. Here, the demands of particular interest groups tend to polarize more violently than in the case of zoning conflicts on an intraurban scale. Within a metropolitan area there are alternative localities which offer an escape from environmental nuisance. But if the few comparatively untouched natural areas of a country are permanently lost, or if the highpoints of a country's scenic heritage are spoilt, nothing can replace them. In Britain, for example, the mining industry's renewed interest in metal-rich Snowdonia National Park—a locality unique for the recreational opportunities it offers a highly urbanized population—aroused intense reactions. In the United States, the highly mineralized areas in the Boulder, White Cloud Peaks, and Pioneer mountains in Idaho have long supported mineral prospecting and mining claims. But in recent years additional exploration has raised the question of what is the highest valued use of the area, one of the most dramatic landscapes in the nation. How are these intangible recreational and scenic benefits to be measured? How, in any balance sheet of policy alternatives, can they be compared with the tangible costs and benefits of mineral exploitation? There are signs that even in this difficult sphere solutions are possible. Social scientists, working with engineers, are trying to develop a methodology which will provide the basis for comparative analysis of such apparently disparate elements and thus assist in public decision making. (23, 24, 37)

Experience gained in controlling limestone aggregate production in or near to urban areas, through zoning and land use regulations, offers many lessons for the broader geographical context within which land use conflicts are now being raised. Especially is this the case in the matter of land rehabilitation. However, it is clear that the current widespread concern in defense of national and international environmental quality poses a number of additional questions of a more complex and controversial nature. The effort to find acceptable answers has only just begun.

THREE · THE SUMMING UP:

in which the principal
determinants of the
patterns of mineral
exploitation and use are
highlighted, and some
continuing uncertainties
are recognized

8 MINERALS IN PERSPECTIVE

HERE, then, is a picture of the mineral industry —its problems and some of the issues that affect it. The picture is by no means complete, but it at least presents a reasonable cross section and gives some idea of industry operations, particularly those of production. It is abundantly clear that the industry is faced with many uncertainties, and it is on these that we shall focus in bringing into perspective the content of the preceding chapters.

If minerals are to be of service to man, they must be moved from their place of origin into the stream of industrial raw materials. On this journey the passage is sometimes easy because of the fortuitous juxtaposition of a reserve near a major metal market, or the availability of low-cost, bulk ocean transport, or the absence of artificial trade barriers. In other instances the passage may be hindered by obstacles, either natural (as when a marginal reserve or a remote location makes the production and transport of a mineral difficult) or artificial (as when a foreign exchange shortage exists in an importing country). On the whole, however, the movement of minerals to their markets works remarkably well, although the routes are sometimes more complex (and more costly) than they would be if the world were a single, smoothly functioning political unit. In regard to the future, however, as global mineral requirements continue to grow it is impossible to predict exactly what mineral reserves will be exploited and which routes mineral raw materials will take to their markets.

Of the variety of interlinked uncertainties clouding that future, some are geological, some are technological, and some are economic; others are environmental and political. As far as the geological uncertainties are concerned, our fundamental assumption is that, because the earth is made of minerals, there exists in general and for the foreseeable future a truly abundant raw material resource base for the mineral industry. However, it must be recognized that the quality of detailed geological information about that resource base on a global scale remains remarkably limited—largely because geological knowledge has been constrained in the past by the relatively small sums spent on explorations into the nature of the earth's crust.

The assurance of a continuous supply of minerals from this relatively unexplored resource base—if indeed that is considered to be desirable—depends in part upon assumptions about the pace of technological advance. Modern technology certainly affords opportunities for discovering more about the geology of the world on a scale and at a pace that was unimagined two or more decades ago; but these opportunities have been only partly grasped. In the fields of mining and beneficiation, and especially in the sphere of smelting and refining, it can be expected that technology will be adjusted and advanced to meet the changing opportunities for mineral exploitation. There is much in the historical experience of the mineral industry to suggest that this is likely to happen. It is the timing and relative costs of different advances that remain open to question.

It has been shown in earlier chapters how historical patterns of mineral supply have been boldly shaped by economic, environmental, and political factors. At all levels of the mineral industry's activity—from the development of a local mine, to the shaping of national mineral policies, to the evolution of global patterns of mineral trade—their importance is fundamental and tending to increase. Combined, their unpredictability provides some of the more fascinating issues in understanding the mineral industry today, and there can be little doubt that these factors pose some of the most difficult questions and some of the largest problems of resource evaluation and mineral use in the future.

Each of these broad areas of uncertainty—geology, technology, economics, environmental issues, and politics—deserves further consideration.

GEOLOGY • In turning first to the uncertainties surrounding the geological occurrence of minerals, the distinction between the known mineral reserves and the global resource base—that is, all mineral materials that exist in the earth—must again be stressed. The mining industry concerns itself primarily with the known, although it also has a strong interest in that part of the unknown which can be developed in the foreseeable future at present cost levels and using present technology. In considering medium- and longer-term resource availabilities, however, one must set horizons well beyond the reserves shown in the reports of mining companies or even in the estimates of government agencies. The very existence of published quantitative estimates of mineral reserves—estimates which, as has been noted, reflect more than anything else the amount of money invested in looking for particular minerals in particular places—gives a somewhat misleading impression of accuracy and finality in these matters, which has given support to those who prophesy mineral shortages. Fortunately, as was noted in several of the commodity studies in Part Two, the overall picture of resource occurrence and availability affords grounds for guarded optimism.

Iron and Steel. In the case of iron ore, reserves are high and the resource picture is one of remarkable abundance, as one would expect from a material that makes up nearly 6 percent of the earth's crust. Supply patterns are changing. While the direct shipping ores of the United States and the Minette ores of Lorraine have lost popularity with the steel industry (perhaps to regain it at some future date), new high-grade ores in Australia, Africa, Asia, and Latin America, and low-grade taconite ores in the United States combine to provide the world's iron and steel industry with an abundant raw material base. World supplies of the more important *alloying elements*—manganese, nickel, chromium, molybdenum, and vanadium—are also known to be potentially available at approximately present prices to meet prospective demands well into the twenty-first century. However, their distribution is such as to pose a number of strategic questions for some of the largest steel-producing nations.

In the weakest position is Japan, followed by the countries of the enlarged European Economic Community. These centers of industrial growth in general are poorly endowed with commercial deposits of the alloying elements. Supply security, therefore, must rest upon diversity of sources, stockpiles, and, where possible, recycling. Although the United States now imports most of its manganese, chromium, and vanadium, as well as considerable quantities of nickel, all these materials could in fact be obtained at somewhat higher costs from domestic sources. The U.S.S.R. is apparently in the strongest position, being designedly self-sufficient and having in addition some ores for sale on the open market. Overall, then, the evidence strongly suggests that any problems that might arise in the provision of alloying elements for the world's iron and steel industry would stem from economic and political blockages in the supply system rather than from any basic deficiency of natural resources.

The Base Metals. Turning to the base metals, the situation is different only in emphasis and detail. In the case of *copper,* many low-grade deposits are being developed in various parts of the world, and there are no grounds for believing that global resources are dangerously low. There is some question, however, as to whether the real price of copper might rise due to the combination of increased mining costs as the grade of ore falls, increased processing costs as the cost of energy rises, and increased taxes and royalties as the producing countries retain a greater share of industry revenue. All of this will have important ramifications on the rate of demand expansion and on substitution.

Lead is less abundant in the earth's crust than copper; yet new reserves have been discovered and developed in recent years to provide what appear to be adequate sources of supply for many years to come, especially if the opportunities for increasing the recovery and use of secondary lead are firmly grasped. *Zinc* is not so easily recycled, and its price has failed to encourage a vigorous search for new supplies in recent years. An apparently weak reserve position in the case of this metal, therefore, must be set alongside the fact that it is more abundant than copper in the earth's crust. Even a modest increase in price would in all likelihood quickly lead to a more favorable reserve position.

The same is true of *tin,* although current geological knowledge would suggest that tin is likely to be a less abundant material. Nevertheless, in many of its present markets the substitution of other metals and materials would be no difficult matter. Consequently, any future scarcity of tin seems more likely to threaten those countries whose economies rest heavily upon its exploitation rather than to pose a fundamentally serious resource problem.

The Light Metals. As to the light metals, with *aluminum* making up some 8 percent of the crust of the earth, resource adequacy is unquestioned. However, technological and economic problems could possibly emerge for the industry in the future. Although bauxite reserves have been increased substantially over the last twenty years or so, and will doubtless be expanded even further, in the longer run it will probably be necessary to find economic technologies based upon alternative raw materials—and preferably technologies that will not use greatly increased quantities of energy per unit of finished metal.

Magnesium is abundant in the earth, and also is technically recoverable from the almost limitless resources of the sea. *Titanium* also poses no resource problems, especially in its lower-grade form of ilmenite. Any problems of supply in the case of these two minor light metals are more likely to stem from shortages of low-cost energy than from a scarcity of the parent raw materials.

Nonmetallic Minerals. The most widely used nonmetallic minerals, the *industrial rocks,* owe their importance in large part to their abundance and frequency of occurrence. Since they make up the earth itself, the resource base is for all practical purposes unlimited and factors other

than occurrence usually determine their exploitability. In the industrial minerals the physical characteristics of the naturally occurring
material are of primary importance. Thus, although the amount of
feldspar or mica or quartz in the crust of the earth is remarkably
large, only material from certain areas is of use to man.

Factors of Demand and Supply. Geological occurrence sets the stage
for mankind's present and prospective mining activities. Despite the
fact that mineral deposits are fixed in location and fixed in size, the
present evidence is that global resources of minerals, which constitute
the resource base, are generously available to meet the needs of many
generations to come. The resource base is the ultimate limitation, and
in probing towards this distant limit the flexibility of the technological,
economic, and political options that are open to man become particularly decisive.

However, one basic limitation cannot be overlooked: the further
we look into the future, the more tentative must be our conclusions.
It is for this reason that many of the forecasts based upon economic
logic and covering a span of no more than forty or fifty years are
somewhat at odds with the ecological school of thought, which tends
to take a longer and on the whole more pessimistic view of resource
availabilities. Over an extended time-scale, demand projections inevitably appear to be more plausible (granted the prospects for worldwide population and economic growth) than supply forecasts. In the
longer run the latter must lean upon technological and market assumptions, which are subject to much greater uncertainty.

By the same token, while the process of substitution in the recent
past can indicate possible and even probable developments in the
next decade and more, in the longer term the quantification of possibilities becomes highly tentative. Longer-term mineral supply forecasts, therefore, legitimately and inevitably are associated with wide
areas of uncertainty which must be recognized even within a context
of cautious optimism.

TECHNOLOGY • For someone who has never lived without electricity,
plumbing, or paved roads (the condition of most farm living only a
little more than a generation ago), the enormous impact of technology
on modern society is sometimes difficult to grasp. The impact of
technological change on the mining industry, however, is somewhat
easier to illustrate and thus is more readily appreciated. Change has
characterized every aspect of the industry, from the search for ore
to the pouring of the metals; and if there is a single theme in this
change it is in the scale of operations—the increased scale of exploration, the increased scale of mine workings, the increased scale of ore
movement, the increased scale of ore refining, and the like. The

exploration phase of the industry, only briefly mentioned earlier, deserves some attention here.

Most mineral deposits occur in bedrock and, although the mineral-bearing zones of the rock may outcrop at the surface of the earth, they are normally buried under varying thicknesses of barren rock, soil, or water. Finding the deposits which show at the surface is relatively easy and—disregarding oil and gas—it is these that have supplied most of the mineral wealth used to date. The early prospectors, who found most of them, were limited to outcropping deposits because they had no techniques for discovering those that were buried.

It is only over the last half century that man has developed approaches and techniques that permit a systematic search over large areas for deposits that do not show at the surface. During this period technology has provided tools and equipment that give a remarkable amount of information about these rocks—about their weight, electrical conductivity and resistance, radioactivity, chemical composition, a whole series of characteristics which the expert can translate into information on the probability of the existence of usable material beneath any part of the earth's surface. Thus the nickel deposits of the Thompson mine in Manitoba were discovered through use of instruments which read the electrical conductivity and magnetic attraction of the underlying rock, the uranium finds of the Colorado Plateau depended upon the use of the Geiger counter, which measures radioactivity, and in highly settled southeastern Pennsylvania, airborne magnetometers probed over 1,500 feet (450 meters) below the surface and detected the iron ore body of the Grace mine, which is within sight of the Pennsylvania Turnpike. These North American examples are repeated many times in other parts of the world. Yet only a fraction of the earth so far has been explored by means of modern techniques. Technology had added a new scale and a third dimension to exploration, greatly increasing the chances of discovering the unknown.

To consider again the commodities that have been discussed earlier in the book, almost every phase of every industry has been radically changed by technological advance. The iron and steel industry, for example, is passing through a major and continuing technological revolution. The nature of iron ore mining is changing with the increasing use of new types or lower grades of material which can be beneficiated and agglommerated to form a high-quality furnace charge. These high-grade feeds in (enlarged) blast furnaces give the ironmaking process more flexibility and lower costs. Similar changes are seen in steelmaking, particularly with the growing use of the basic oxygen converter, which has placed a premium upon low-phosphorus pig iron and iron ore—much to the disadvantage of the Swedish industry. Simultaneously, the construction of ever-larger integrated plants has given a new value to those places where raw materials can be efficiently assembled near to the largest industrial markets. This in turn has revised the value of some ore deposits, and has afforded new opportunities to producers with easy access to deep water. Other new processes, such as the direct reduction of ore with natural gas in Mexico, have given an unexpected value to particular ore deposits in particular places. The location as well as the scale of the iron and steel industry, therefore, is in a remarkably fluid state in large measure because of technological advance, and this situation seems likely to persist into the future.

The alloying elements that are in good supply are in many instances the products of a special technical effort. By-product production of molybdenum, vanadium, and a variety of other materials provides a case where the infeasible has been turned into the feasible by means of technology. Where domestic supplies are short or foreign supplies subject to severe fluctuations, technology tends to be at its most ingenious, especially in such "continental economies" as the United States or the U.S.S.R. Thus, the substitution of molybdenum for tungsten, of aluminum for tin, and of ceramics for refractory metals all reveal the importance of technology. Similarly, research into the recovery of mineral materials from unconventional sources—such as the possibility of recovering manganese from nodules on the sea bottom—demonstrates its potential. Apparently this latter source offers no insurmountable technological obstacle, but it is doubtful if it would ever have been considered if the United States had possessed adequate domestic resources of manganese from conventional sources.

The copper industry, too, reflects a triumph of technology, for its present reserves include grades of material which not so long ago were well down in the resources category or perhaps even in the resource base. In the case of lead and zinc, the development of extensive, low-grade bodies might become technologically and economically feasible in due course. With all of the base metals, as with most other metals, research is being conducted simultaneously on a number of levels. While one group of research activities is directed towards the development of processes that will allow the exploitation of low-grade deposits to increase mineral supplies, other workers are attempting to develop new processes involving new uses for these materials, thereby enlarging their market. In the case of tin, for example, research groups supported by tin producers are trying to develop new uses for the metal; meanwhile, with the security of long-range tin supply in some doubt, consumers are developing techniques that would let them reduce their tin requirements.

From the viewpoint of technology, the light metal industries might well be looked upon as a part of the chemical industry rather than the mineral industry. Indeed, as the mining industry moves toward progressively lower-grade raw materials, and as the base from which such materials are drawn becomes broader, the role of "mining" as a fine art declines; the emphasis shifts to processing, which can be carried on at places divorced from the mine. Thus, the day is approaching when mining will become little more than the initial, rock-moving stage of a series of chemical processes that feed raw materials to industry. Its character will then be much more akin to the present-day nonmetallic mineral industry, which in recent years has pioneered the development of heavy earth-moving equipment, of scrapers, loaders, draglines, and the like. Together, these have revolutionized the mining of industrial rocks and greatly increased the range of usable materials. Companies in this sector of the mining industry— for example, cement companies or aggregate producers in urban areas—annually handle millions of tons of raw materials, and were among the first to move towards automated operations and an extensive use of electronic computers in mining, marketing, and the administrative part of their operations.

In parenthesis, mention can be made of one aspect of technology which has affected the nonmetallic minerals and which can in a sense reduce mineral reserves. This is the production of synthetic minerals. In the case of certain nonmetallic minerals such as diamonds, quartz crystals, graphite, and mica, modern man has succeeded in doing what the alchemist was never able to do for gold: he has succeeded in replicating those physical characteristics that make them of value to industry. In some cases the synthetic material can be produced at costs equivalent to the natural product. Here technology revolutionizes the world resource picture and a further fall in the costs of the synthetic material in effect forces the shift of the natural reserves back into the resources category. Similarly, technological developments in recycling offer additional possibilities for extending reserves.

Possibilities for the Future. To the present, technology not only has served to encourage a greater use of mineral raw materials, but has simultaneously helped to provide the larger reserves that are required. In the future, technology will doubtless play much the same role, although it remains uncertain how the timing and cost of technological advance will affect particular minerals and particular deposits. There are some aspects of broad technological developments that offer some concern for the future, however. Two of these stem from the superior economics of strip mining by comparison with underground workings: the environmental impact of modern mining techniques (a subject to which we shall return later in this chapter) and the question of energy supplies.

As the mining industry has turned to progressively lower grades of ore, entailing the use of larger machines to remove greater quantities of material for a given amount of metal, the energy employed per unit of metal output has steadily increased. There have been restraints, of course. Through improvements in some of its larger machines, the industry is using energy more efficiently; nevertheless, the mineral industry's trend towards increased energy consumption raises several important questions for its future. First, because energy production is a source of active and troublesome residuals, the more the minerals industry uses the greater will be its indirect contribution to environmental stresses and the more, therefore, will it be affected by measures designed to reduce those stresses. Second, when energy becomes a major factor in producing metal products, low-cost sources of power become a major factor bearing on the location of the mineral industry. This could influence the longer-term geography of the industry to a degree not yet discernible. Third, there is the question of energy availability.

Opinions are divided as to the adequacy of medium- and longer-term energy supplies, particularly with regard to the prospective supply of oil and natural gas. Apart from the question of physical availability, it is apparent that a variety of political and institutional factors playing upon the international market for oil in particular can seriously disrupt supplies and prices to the energy-deficient industrial zones of the world. These disturbances in the oil market affect the real price of energy and, in turn, the cost structure of those industries heavily reliant upon large quantities of energy.

It is important not to be overwhelmed by the price instability and supply uncertainty of the early 1970s—much can happen to influence energy prospects during the next few years. At the same time, the cost and availability of future alternative energy supplies are unknowns in the calculations of the mining and smelting industries, and will have an uncertain influence on their prospective behavior.

ECONOMICS • All mineral producers operate within a distinctive economic framework, which varies between different industries and between different countries. In the commodity discussions we have noted many ways in which economic forces shape the behavior of the mineral industry. For example, the contrasts between totally different political and economic systems—especially between the market economies and the fully-planned Communist economies—and their effects upon the size, location, and style of the mineral industry in different parts of the world, were mentioned in the discussion of the concept of mineral resources (chap. 5). These contrasts are especially obvious in the objectives and cost allocations of mineral exploration.

The discussion of the alloys and the base metals (chaps. 4 and 5) noted the implications of mineral by-production and co-production.

From this it is seen how difficult it would be to assess, say, American reserves of molybdenum or vanadium, for most of them are not reserves of molybdenum or vanadium in their own right. It might be possible to appraise the molybdenum ore reserves at Climax, Colorado; however, this would have meaning only if by-production of copper ores does not increase significantly. Similarly, the by-product content of ores cannot strictly be considered as a reserve or as a resource, except as it relates to the minerals with which it is produced. For although it is technologically feasible to produce just molybdenum from copper ores, to do so would be grossly uneconomic.

In comments on the changes in iron ore flows and in the discussion of the aluminum industry (chaps. 3 and 6) we stressed the response of the mining industry to differences in transport costs and freight rates—and the outstanding attractiveness of low-cost, ocean bulk transport. Sometimes the rates charged for transport reflect, more than anything else, distance and vessel operating costs; other times, however, the rates charged for particular hauls bear a stronger relationship to other factors, with the result that they afford surprising advantages to particular mineral deposits. Back-hauls of iron ore from West Africa to the United States are a case in point, as are the effects of discriminatory maritime legislation. Mexican sulfur, for example, has a transport cost advantage over Texas output in the East Coast market of the United States because it can be shipped at low international freight rates; in contrast, coastwise traffic between American ports is administered under the 1921 Merchant Marine Act, which demands that trade be handled only in the relatively high-cost vessels of American companies, which in turn are required to sail vessels built in American yards and manned by American crews.

For several minerals the importance of substitution was underlined (chaps. 4 and 6). The effects of this economic process can be indirect as well as direct. In the past, for example, despite the limited number of known nickel deposits in the world, the main nickel producer in North America faced substantial competition from other materials which can be substituted for that metal, and this characteristic has placed constraints upon the pricing policy of the International Nickel Company of Canada, Ltd. (The supply of nickel is now changing, however, with the advent of technology enabling a new type of deposit, the laterites, to be developed in new producing areas such as Australia and Indonesia.)

In the case of tin we noted the possible effects of price fluctuations upon the organization of a metal market. Tin also served to stress the importance of mineral exports for the economies of many producing countries. In such cases, and especially in the developing world, efforts to stabilize prices may be an important aspect of external assistance, for in some countries a decrease in mineral export prices can more than offset all the foreign aid credits that many of those countries receive.

All these and many other economic responses provide an essential vantage point for viewing the future of the minerals industry. But for some areas the impact of economic forces remains poorly explored; hence their future impacts are unpredictable. One such area is the captive mine; another is the evaluation of risk.

Captive Mines and the Assessment of Risk. In the cases of both the iron ore and the chromium industries the mineral industry responded to the possibility of disrupted supplies by instituting the vertical integration of ore and metal production. The captive mines in distant lands which belong to the large producers of ferrochrome in the United States serve as an example of the thousands of mineral properties that were developed by foreign capital under quite a different economic environment than prevails today.

The establishment of mines in foreign countries involves much more than the purchase of mineral-bearing properties. International mining companies are often expected to maintain standards well above those of domestic companies operating in the same areas. They must frequently invest in housing, roads, power plants, transportation facilities, recreation facilities, and a host of services which contribute to the mining operation through contributing to the welfare of the miners. In many cases these heavy financial commitments must be made in parts of the world where the political risks are relatively high. In the past, major international mining companies have felt that the assured steady supply of material to be expected from a captive mine more than compensates for any increase in cost. This is a difficult situation to assess. Its logic rests partly upon the fact that mining is only the first step in a series of operations, and any disturbance in the flow of raw materials can disrupt the whole series. In the case of chromite, a shortage might extend to the final stage of production of certain alloy steels in which chrome is essential. Thus the assurance provided by captive production may warrant this type of operation, but at the same time the risk of unfavorable changes in the political and economic climate in producing countries could well lead to the evolution of alternative means of securing a steady supply of minerals.

This highlights one of the most important aspects of a mineral investment decision, the assessment of the various types of risk involved. After completing all the calculations preceding an investment (size of the ore body, cost of production, expense of processing, freight rates to the markets, size of prospective contracts, and the like) and assuming a reasonable rate of return upon the investment has been indicated, a mining company must squarely face the evaluation of risks.

Risks, of course, surround virtually every phase of the mining industry. Geological tests can be deceptive; concentrator or smelter technology may turn out to be troublesome; the freight market may harden and rates rise; the market for the product may soften and prices fall. And risks exist that the political environment of the mining operation will change, through a change in government or the demonstration effect of mineral expropriations elsewhere in the world. This last is reflected in two of the more impressive features of the mineral industry in the last decade: first, the search in many mineral consuming countries for additional domestic minerals; and, second, a preference for investment in such countries as Canada and Australia, which have outstanding records of political stability.

A decade ago, Australia was a minor element on the international mineral scene. By 1970, however, the country produced 51 million tons of iron ore, 9 million tons of bauxite, 1.3 million tons of titanium ores, 750,000 tons of manganese, and increasing quantities of copper, zinc, lead, tin, and nickel (table 19). A large share of this production was for export. In large measure, this remarkable record is a function of the country's geology. But growth is also a response to changing technology, particularly in the transport sector, and to the decreasing relative isolation of Australia. A changing attitude on the part of the Australian government towards mineral exports has also contributed. But after linking together all these elements, it is clear that the growth of the Australian mineral industry is a measure of the relatively low political risks involved in mineral investment there by comparison with many other geographical alternatives. In the Australian achievement, too, it is possible to see clearly the considerable overlap between economic and political factors that influence the behavior and constrain the future options of the mineral industry.

ENVIRONMENTAL ISSUES • A pervading element throughout this book has been the direct and indirect effects that activities of the mining industry may have upon the environment and, inversely, the effects that environmental issues may have upon the way in which the industry operates. In chapter 5, for example, the discussion of lead touched on opportunities for recycling metals—and also on the possible effects on the lead market of antipollution regulations involving decreased use of lead as a gas additive. In chapter 7, when dealing with sulfur, it was shown how concern for a deteriorating environment has succeeded in increasing sulfur supplies to the point of potential glut. Later in that chapter consideration of limestone emphasized some continuing conflicts in land use—mineral development versus alternative uses—which await resolution. Sometimes the pressures of environmental concern increase mineral supply; sometimes they decrease it.

TABLE 19
Australian production and exports
of minerals, 1966 and 1970
(thousand tons)

	1966 Production	1966 Exports	1970 Production	1970 Exports
Bauxite	1,827	873	9,388	3,400
Copper*	111	15	151	37
Iron ore	11,738	343	51,104	34
Lead*	371	69	457	90
Manganese	318	70	752	649
Nickel*	—	—	29	—
Sulfur*	265	59	320	124
Tin*	5	1	9	4
Titanium†	770	597	1,257	1,032
Zinc*	375	142	489	235

Source: Institute of Geological Sciences (22).
 * Metal content.
 † Ilmenite, rutile, and leucoxene.

A Focus on National and Local Issues. In a sense, environmental concerns and policies affecting mineral supply are a subset of the political factors discussed in the next section of this chapter. They are treated separately here mainly for two reasons. First, although environmental issues sometimes do have an international dimension (as was stressed by the United Nations' 1972 Conference on the Human Environment), their essential focus is at local and national levels. Second, particularly in the industrially developed countries increasing populations and higher income levels have generated, on the one hand, greater demands for minerals and, on the other, a growing awareness of the need for space, beauty, recreation, and tranquility to balance the pressures and strictures imposed by the acquisition of material goods.

In addition, there is a possibility that the increasing scale of mining operations and the tendency to mine larger quantities of progressively lower-grade ores to produce a given tonnage of metal could lead to localized yet severe environmental damage in some parts of the world. For example, in the western United States ores are mined bearing a mere 0.6 percent of copper. In one sense this is a triumph of technology, but it leads to a great deal of waste material. With overburden also having to be removed, this can result in the removal of 500 tons of earth in order to produce a ton of copper. In addition, of course, the ore has to be concentrated before it is smelted, which means that about 99 percent of the ore has to be removed as "tailings." Problems of water and air pollution also occur, since the concentrators and refiners are rarely environmentally neutral, and often the tailings are carried into streams and smelter gases and dust are blown into the air.

All of this environmental damage is far from inevitable, and in the United States and Europe concerned governmental agencies have taken serious steps to eliminate it. The mines can be landscaped and their overburden planted. The concentrators can be made more efficient and the tailings can be moved as a slurry to suitable locations for stabilization. And smelters can be improved to reduce the amount of objectionable gases in their emissions. Such palliatives, however, demand huge capital investments and impose additional major operating costs. Whether these additional costs can be sustained will vary from mineral to mineral, and from mine to mine. The industry as a whole, however, is awakening to the fact that in the future it will be required to internalize costs which previously devolved on the community in general, and this is bound to influence its relative competitiveness against producers in countries where concern for the environment has not yet become a controlling issue.

Public intervention in the behavior of the mineral industries on environmental grounds is designed essentially to protect or restore the quality of the environment, at the same time as providing for the material needs of mankind. The objective is to try to ensure that the industry concerned—be it an iron ore mine or an integrated steelworks, a limestone quarry or a zinc smelter—minimizes its impact upon the physical environment and operates within a framework of publicly accepted standards. These standards clearly stem from a set of environmental priorities, which begin with the need to ensure human health and safety, and subsequently to consider economic and environmental health as measured by various biological and social parameters. Lower in the order of priorities tend to come various land use planning considerations, followed by attempts (as yet very tentative) to ensure "the conservation of material and environmental resources through technological assessment and prudent use of substitute and recyclable materials." (37, p. 71)

Much of the attention of government environmental agencies in the developed world in recent years has been directed towards the control of pollution. This is the most easily monitored nuisance. It can readily be reduced. And the policy is addressed to the first of the environmental priorities—the need to ensure human health and safety. In the longer term, however, it will be desirable to focus upon broader policies of environmental management in order to satisfy more effectively the changing needs of society. It is this prospective shift of emphasis in environmental concerns and policies—differing, as it well may, among the countries of the world—that provides us with some puzzling complexities about future mineral developments.

POLITICS • A review of the pattern of world mineral supply highlights the high degree of interdependence among nations. The United States has little manganese or chrome or graphite, but in the world there is plenty. Russia is not well endowed with copper or molybdenum, but in the world there is plenty. The great industrial complexes of the European Economic Community and Japan must rely on outside sources for a great part of their mineral raw materials, but there is no risk that they will go short unless there is disruption in the channels of international commerce.

On all levels—local, national, and global—political forces influence and sometimes control mineral development. The logic of these forces may at times be questioned; the mechanisms adopted are often imperfect; and the results are sometimes different from what was intended. Yet the fundamental validity of political constraints on the mineral industry and mineral development cannot be challenged. The challenge exists rather in the need to harmonize the goals and interests of those concerned with mineral production— mainly the producers who control the physical deposits, and the governments that shape the political environment in which production and consumption take place—in order to ensure that these resources of the earth are developed in the best interests of the earth's inhabitants.

The final consumer or user of a mineral is rarely involved in political matters (except in the case of captive or integrated production). He is primarily interested in obtaining a material, be it tin or lead or paper or plastic, which will perform a particular function. If this material happens to be tin, he is not concerned whether the tin is Malaysian or Bolivian. If it is lead, he is not concerned whether it comes from Yugoslavia or Idaho so long as he can count on getting the amounts he needs at the right time and at a price he can afford. He rarely has a political preference as to their source. To the consuming nation, however, all sources are not equal. As has been noted, political blocs and economic groupings, tariff barriers and balance of payment problems, barter agreements and foreign aid objectives, and a host of other political constraints bear heavily upon trading patterns in minerals and metals. It is in this area that many uncertainties of mineral supply are encountered.

The Local Level. There are questions and problems of mineral production that are political in nature even on the local level, of course. To some extent these foreshadowed the current widespread concern over the way in which man deals with his environment, and it has been the nonmetallic mineral industries of the developed countries that have had to face most frequently the realities of political considerations. As affluence has increased so have political priorities become more noticeable, to add a further complication to the assessment of reserves and resources.

Take the case of such prosaic materials as limestone and gravel (discussed in chap. 7) which are used in enormous quantities in constructing the roads and buildings of highly populated areas. Where within the reserves–resources–resource-base concept (figure 8) would it be appropriate to place a limestone or gravel deposit, which could be commercially developed using present technology but which cannot be developed because the people in adjoining areas do not wish to have a neighboring pit or quarry? Here the obstacles are more than environmental. The obstacles to mineral development are economic (the desire to maintain property values) and social (community attitudes towards an appropriate residential environment). If the pressures of society lead to a decision to do without this specific deposit and to get the mineral from a more distant and more expensive source, the limestone or the gravel found in this location could under no circumstances be considered as a reserve. The recovery of minerals in such an instance is considered as one of several possible forms of land use, and other uses take precedence.

Although this situation is particularly associated with heavily settled areas, it is becoming increasingly important in other localities where the mineral industry operates, most noticeably in areas of natural beauty such as national parks. Mining interests may be less than enthusiastic about such political constraints, but their growing importance has greatly increased the industry's awareness of environmental issues and has led to a much more careful planning of new development.

Producing and Consuming Countries. It is at the national level, however, that political attitudes and actions are the most influential. In the technically simple process of moving mineral raw materials from the place where they are produced to the place where they are consumed, there are many diverse interests—not only of producers and consumers, but also of producing countries and consuming countries—to complicate and sometimes disrupt the flows. In recent decades the role of the producing or host country has become much more critical with the emergence of new nations which are major suppliers of raw materials and which in turn rely heavily on the contribution of natural resource exploitation in their economic development.

A common objective of such a producing country must be to get as high a financial return from its minerals as possible. But this is not the only goal, and perhaps it should not be the primary one. A major objective in many cases should be to use mineral development as a springboard to improve the country's standard of living. There have been many changes in approach and thinking on the role of minerals in developing economies over recent decades, and there can be no single answer to how it can best be dealt with.

Should a developing nation allow its mineral resources to be developed by international industry to feed the raw material appetites of the industrial countries? This would be a continuation of past policy, with the significant difference that today the producing country has much more to say about the conditions under which production takes place, and about the benefits which remain in the country. If an equitable division of benefits can be arrived at, the developing country may receive large amounts of foreign exchange from mineral exports plus significant improvements in its infrastructure (roads, ports, power, etc.). If the foreign exchange is wisely employed, it can play an important part in the economic development of the country. This policy has been followed by such countries as Canada, where the production and export of minerals and other raw materials have been important factors in the country's economic development. Can the less developed countries emulate it?

Alternatively, a developing nation could attempt to develop its own mineral resources and then place them on the world market. A number of countries are doing this, either through nationalizing existing industries or restricting operations to national companies. This approach assumes the availability of the large amounts of capital needed to develop or maintain a mining operation. And considering the risks involved and the long pay-off period, it is uncertain whether this is the best use of the domestic or external assistance capital of a developing country.

There are many ways in which such a country can make use of its limited capital resources in order to make a more immediate impact on its living standards—the construction of roads, schools, fertilizer plants, textile mills, and the like. For many of these purposes private foreign capital is simply not available and funds must be raised internally or must come from development grants and loans. But somewhere in the world there always seems to be private capital available for the development of a good mineral deposit—capital which would not come into the country for any other purpose. There appears to be much logic to the country tapping this considerable, albeit inflexible, source of capital—for the interests of the international mining industry and the developing countries are not fundamentally divergent.

Should a developing nation leave its mineral resources in the ground, saving them for the future use of its own people? This is a policy advocated by some countries, and it has a basic appeal since mineral deposits do not spoil and they can be developed anytime in the future. But there are two obvious disadvantages. First, since minerals are of no real value until they are mined, the country following this policy denies itself current wealth as well as the economic and social benefits which mineral development, properly handled, can bring to its people. Second, although mineral deposits do not change, the climate in which they are used does. A deposit considered rich today may become worthless if better sources are discovered, if new use patterns come into being, or if a cheap substitute is developed. For example, given the present economics of iron ore mining and beneficiation, plus the preferences of the steel industry's blast furnace managers, it is highly unlikely that the Schefferville development on the Quebec-Labrador boundary in Canada (which delivered its first direct shipping ore in 1954) would be initiated in the 1970s.

The normal response to these questions—as is often the case in questions of politics—involves elements of compromise. In many cases, international mineral producers and host governments are today arriving at special agreements (long-term leases, production sharing, joint-ventures, etc.) which give the host country generous access to international mining capital and technology. Such agreements also allow the host country to exercise appropriate control over the politically weighted aspects of mineral development. At the same time the producing company is afforded suitable production and marketing rights.

Developing Countries as Consumers. No consideration of future mineral supply patterns can be complete without some mention of the developing nations—not only the mineral producers, but all countries of the Third World—as potential mineral consumers. Today, they use minerals in very limited quantities. The average Indian in 1971 used about 31 pounds (14 kilograms) of steel, compared with an American's 1,360 pounds (617 kilograms). Rapidly developing Mexico used less than 2 pounds of aluminum per person, compared with America's 49 pounds. If each individual in the world were to have allotted to him as much steel, or copper, or aluminum as was used on the average by each individual in the United States, at 1971 rates this would require a threefold increase in world production of steel and copper and an increase of almost 6½ times in production of aluminum. It is doubtful that each individual in the world will either need or want as much as this, but one thing is clear: he wants a good deal more than he is receiving today.

The fulfillment of these needs, which on any basis are phenomenally large, has seldom been taken into account in past reckoning, and is seldom taken into account in today's planning. Such figures have no imminent reality but they do express a level of aspiration and bear upon political attitudes in some parts of the world.

Imports and Self-Sufficiency. Political considerations also enter into the behavior of the more highly industrial nations, varying not only with the basic political-economic philosophy of their governments

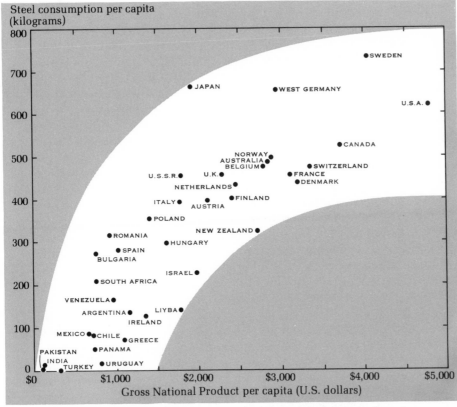

Figure 14. United Nations data for 1971 show a close relationship between a country's gross national product and its consumption of steel. *Source:* United Nations (44).

but also with the degree of mineral self-sufficiency the countries have been able to achieve. The United States provides a particularly interesting case, for with less than 6 percent of the world's population, the country consumes about one quarter of its minerals. The United States is a major user of minerals, in part at least, because it has been fortunate enough to have major deposits of most of the essential minerals within its borders and in adjacent friendly countries. These resources have been expended freely and sometimes recklessly. In building up the American economy, the best of them have been used up. True, there still are abundant resources of a somewhat lower grade to be used, but some of these cost more to produce than minerals purchased on the world market.

Where should the United States go from here? Any number of choices exist, for there are many ways in which the country's mineral needs can be met. As has been noted, mineral users normally have no preferences and would like to get the bulk of their supplies from the cheapest source, which in many cases is abroad. Foreign producers, often affiliated with American companies, would agree with this. Domestic producers, of course, favor domestic production, even if this involves some form of subsidy or restriction on imports. They point out the dangers of being too reliant on foreign sources of critical materials, and the problems that arise in domestic mining areas if the industry is allowed to decline. If domestic sources are favored, it may be necessary to pay more. Nevertheless, such a policy would give the United States a large mining industry which could serve in times when foreign sources are cut off; it would also provide income to remote sections of the country where there are few resources other than minerals; and it would give employment to the people who rely on mining for a living. At the same time, through making domestic mines more attractive and profitable than they would otherwise be, capital and labor, which might be more productively employed in other parts of the economy, would be diverted into mining. The production and environmental costs could be high. From it all, an unspecified degree of security would be gained. Within a very different political-economic framework this would appear to be the policy being followed by the U.S.S.R.

Alternatively, the United States could increasingly purchase minerals on the world market at world prices. Under these conditions there would be some changes in the country's supply pattern. However, the bulk of American mineral material now coming from domestic sources would continue to come from those same sources, for the country still has many rich deposits of a wide variety of minerals that are competitive with any in the world. Some domestic deposits would suffer; but in the main these would be small and marginal, destined to go out of production in any case unless given special support.

In point of fact, government policy towards mineral supply in the United States steers a fluctuating course between these two extremes. Policy varies from mineral to mineral; it is seldom either completely restrictive or completely free; it varies through time. Whether in each case it serves national interests in the most appropriate manner is a matter for continuing debate.

Minerals as a Force in Economic Development. Mineral problems on the international level have probably always existed, but they have come into much finer focus in recent years. An examination of the structure and activities of the mineral industry in the days before World War II reveals a politically fragmented Western Europe and the United States as major consumers of minerals, although in smaller quantities than today. Then, Western Europe was self-sufficient to a much greater degree than it is at present, and the United States was able to supply the bulk of its needs, including all of its iron ore and copper, from domestic sources. Much of the mineral material from other parts of the world entering world trade was produced by foreign subsidiaries of European or American companies, and often it was produced in areas under the political or economic control of industrial countries. Mineral supply functioned smoothly within the economic framework of the time. The consumers and consuming countries were in rather complete control.

In the years since World War II this situation has changed drastically. The major consuming areas in North America, the European Economic Community, and Japan have greatly increased their mineral needs and their degree of reliance on nondomestic sources (the Soviet Union is the major exception here). At the same time the major producing areas outside of the developed countries have either gained their political independence or asserted their economic independence, and are playing a much more decisive role in determining mineral supply patterns. In consequence, mineral production is being more closely tied to the development of the producing country. In this new situation, political and economic relationships have both tended to become much more fluid between the producing and consuming countries, and a new source of uncertainty has been added to the organization of mineral supply. It is this uncertainty that has particularly favored investment in such countries as Australia, Canada, and, to a lesser extent, South Africa during the last decade or more.

Patterns of mineral supply, therefore, are characterized by continuing change as new approaches evolve to improve the relationship between mining companies and their host countries. Mining companies, often part of large international corporations, are today taking a much more constructive approach to their role as partners in the total development of the countries in which they operate. As is also true in the case of environmental issues, this does not represent fundamental changes in the philosophy of the mining industry—any sudden awakening to the fact that past practices were less than ideal. Rather, it represents a normal adjustment to economic and political forces in a competitive world. As Chandler Morse pointed out, private enterprise is neither socially responsible nor irresponsible but rather is a-responsible, since its basic objectives are commercial rather than social. (35, p. 408)

But as the new patterns develop whereby mining companies can integrate their objectives as closely as is economically practical with the broader development and political objectives of the host country (training of personnel, development of roads and power facilities, local provision of materials and supplies), benefits become apparent on both sides indicating that a high level of social responsibility is part of a sound economic structure. Mining is one of the major industries in many developing countries; the contribution it can make in the host country has seldom been fully analyzed, but recent trends seem to point to a greater awareness of the opportunities for mutual benefit possible in the changing relationships between producing and consuming countries.

Thus mineral development involves much more than finding sources of raw materials and moving them towards the market. It demands in addition the creation of a durable political relationship between the sources and consumers of minerals in various parts of the world. This relationship needs to assure a smooth flow of raw materials to the consumers; to offer adequate rewards for producers, investors, and the host country; and to give some thought to the needs of the future.

Today, in many spheres, the world is becoming effectively smaller. Certainly, there is much organized activity through international organizations to remove many of the obstacles to natural resource development and smooth commercial relationships between nations. It is a world, therefore, in which the problems posed by an irregular distribution of the most attractive mineral resources could become progressively less important. It is a world also in which technology is both powerful and ubiquitous enough to transform the mineral supply position of a region, a country, or a bloc—provided the price can be paid. Simultaneously, the strongest economic forces are encouraging the widening of market areas and the integration of economies. In consequence, the mechanisms of political expression and the modes of political activity have taken on fresh importance in recent years. No interpretation of the mineral industry can afford to neglect this global trend of events. No forecast of prospective mineral supplies and trade can ignore its associated uncertainties. But if the peoples of the world continue to work closely together and to move towards an ever more efficient pattern of resource use, those uncertainties will be mitigated and mineral shortages will continue to be only a faint cloud on the world's horizon.

References

1. Agricola. *De Re Metallica* (Hoover translation). New York: Dover, 1950.
2. Brobst, Donald, and Walden P. Pratt, eds. *United States Mineral Resources*, Geological Survey Professional Paper 820. Washington: Government Printing Office, 1973.
3. Brooks, David B. *Low-Grade and Nonconventional Sources of Manganese*. Washington: Resources for the Future, Inc., 1966.
4. ——. *Supply and Competition in Minor Metals*. Washington: Resources for the Future, Inc., 1966.
5. Brown, Harrison. *The Challenge of Man's Future*. New York: Viking Press, 1954.
6. Brubaker, Sterling. *Trends in the World Aluminum Industry*. Baltimore: Johns Hopkins Press for Resources for the Future, Inc., 1967.
7. ——. *To Live on Earth: Man and His Environment in Perspective*. Baltimore: Johns Hopkins University Press for Resources for the Future, Inc., 1972.
8. Buck, W. K., and R. B. Elver. *The Canadian Steel Industry: A Pattern of Growth*. Ottawa: Mineral Information Bulletin, M R 70, Department of Mines and Technical Surveys, 1963.
9. Bureau of Mines (United States). *Mineral Facts and Problems, 1970*. Washington: Government Printing Office, 1972.
10. Bureau of Mines (United States). *Minerals Yearbook, 1970, Volume 1*. Washington: Government Printing Office, 1972.
11. Court, Charles W. M. "International Significance of Mining Development and Overseas Investment." *Mining Congress Journal*. July 1970.
12. Department of Energy, Mines and Resources (Canada). *Canadian Minerals Yearbook 1970*. Ottawa: Information Canada, 1972.
13. Department of the Environment (Britain). *Sinews for Survival*. London: Her Majesty's Stationery Office, 1972.
14. *Electromet Metals and Alloys Review* (Union Carbide Corp.). Vol. II, no. 1, 1959.
15. *Engineering and Mining Journal*. New York, monthly.
16. Faber, M. L. O., and J. G. Potter. *Towards Economic Independence: Papers of the Nationalisation of the Copper Industry in Zambia*. Cambridge (England): University Press, 1971.
17. Fisher, Joseph L., and Neal Potter. *World Prospects for Natural Resources: Some Projections of Demand and Indicators of Supply to the Year 2000*. Washington: Resources for the Future, Inc., 1964.
18. Flawn, Peter T. *Mineral Resources*. Chicago: Rand McNally, 1966.
19. Hazleton, Jared E. *The Economics of the Sulphur Industry*. Washington: Resources for the Future, Inc., 1970.
20. Herfindahl, Orris C. *Copper Costs and Prices: 1870–1957*. Baltimore: Johns Hopkins Press for Resources for the Future, Inc., 1959.
21. ——. *Mineral Import and Stabilization Policies* (Reprint No. 36). Washington: Resources for the Future, Inc., 1962 (out of print).
22. Institute of Geological Sciences. *Statistical Summary of the Mineral Industry, 1966–1970*. London: Her Majesty's Stationery Office, 1972.
23. Kneese, Allen V., and Blair T. Bower, eds. *Environmental Quality Analysis: Theory and Method in the Social Sciences*. Baltimore: Johns Hopkins University Press for Resources for the Future, Inc., 1972.
24. Krutilla, John V., ed. *Natural Environments: Studies in Theoretical and*

Applied Analysis. Baltimore: Johns Hopkins University Press for Resources for the Future, Inc., 1972.

25. Landsberg, Hans H., Leonard L. Fischman, and Joseph L. Fisher. *Resources in America's Future.* Baltimore: Johns Hopkins Press for Resources for the Future, Inc., 1963.

26. Landsberg, Hans H. *Natural Resources for U.S. Growth: A Look Ahead to the Year 2000.* Baltimore: Johns Hopkins Press for Resources for the Future, Inc., 1964.

27. Manners, Gerald. *The Changing World Market for Iron Ore, 1950–1980: An Economic Geography.* Baltimore: Johns Hopkins Press for Resources for the Future, Inc., 1971.

28. ——. *The Changing World Market for Iron Ore: A Descriptive Supplement Covering the Years 1950–1965.* Ann Arbor: University Microfilms (Xerox), 1971.

29. ——. *The Geography of Energy.* London: Hutchinson University Press; second edition, 1972.

30. *Metal Bulletin.* London, weekly.

31. *Metal Bulletin Handbook.* London, annually.

32. Mikesell, Raymond F., and others. *Foreign Investment in the Petroleum and Mineral Industries: Case Studies of Investor-Host Country Relations.* Baltimore: Johns Hopkins Press for Resources for the Future, Inc., 1971.

33. Mineral Resources Consultative Committee (Britain). *Sand and Gravel.* London: Her Majesty's Stationery Office, 1972.

34. *Mining Journal.* London, weekly. (*Annual Review,* each June).

35. Morse, Chandler. "Potentials and Hazards of Direct International Investment in Raw Materials," in *Natural Resources and International Development* (Marion Clawson, ed.). Baltimore: Johns Hopkins Press for Resources for the Future, Inc., 1964.

36. Mumford, Lewis. *Technics and Civilization.* New York: Harcourt, Brace, & World, Inc., 1934.

37. National Academy of Sciences–National Academy of Engineering. *Man, Materials, and Environment: A Report for the National Commission on Materials Policy.* Washington: National Academy of Sciences–National Academy of Engineering, 1973.

38. Netschert, Bruce C., and Hans H. Landsberg. *The Future Supply of the Major Metals.* Washington: Resources for the Future, Inc., 1961 (out of print).

39. Potter, Neal, and Francis T. Christy, Jr. *Trends in Natural Resource Commodities: Statistics of Prices, Output, Consumption, Foreign Trade, and Employment in the United States, 1870–1959.* Baltimore: Johns Hopkins Press for Resources for the Future, 1962.

40. President's Materials Policy Commission. *Resources for Freedom, Volume II.* Washington: Government Printing Office, 1952.

41. *Report of the Commission on Mining and the Environment.* London: Commission on Mining and the Environment, 1972.

42. Schurr, Sam H., and others. *Energy in the American Economy, 1850–1975.* Baltimore: Johns Hopkins Press for Resources for the Future, Inc., 1960.

43. Skinner, Brian J. *Earth Resources.* Englewood Cliffs, N.J.: Prentice-Hall, 1969.

44. United Nations. *Statistical Yearbook 1971.* New York: United Nations, 1972.

45. United States Tariff Commission. *Lead and Zinc.* Tariff Commission Publication 58, May 1962.

46. ——. *Manganese.* Tariff Commission Publication 68, August 1962.
47. Yip Yat Hoong. *The Development of the Tin Mining Industry of Malaya.* Kuala Lumpur: University of Malaya Press, 1969.
48. Zimmerman, Erich W. *World Resources and Industries.* New York: Harper & Row, revised edition, 1951.

Index

THE JOHNS HOPKINS UNIVERSITY PRESS
This book was composed in Linotype Optima text and
Lydian Bold display by the Monotype Composition
Company from a design by Susan Bishop. It was printed
by The Maple Press Company on 60# Publishers Eggshell
Wove. The covers were printed on Columbia Apollo
cloth by The John D. Lucas Printing Company, and the
books were bound by The Maple Press Company.

Library of Congress Cataloging in Publication Data

McDivitt, James Frederick, 1921–
  Minerals and men.
  Bibliography: p.
  1. Mines and mineral resources. 2. Mineral industries. I.
Manners, Gerald, joint author. II. Resources for the Future. III.
Title.
TN19.M2 1974   338.2   73-8138
ISBN 0-8018-1536-3